Navigating Teen Mental Health

An Expert's Guide for Parents

Navigating Teen Mental Health

An Expert's Guide for Parents

Tyish Hall Brown, PhD, MHS

PARENT **READY.**

PARENT **READY**.

Parent Ready
8 East Windsor Avenue
Alexandria, Virginia 22301
https://parentready.com

Copyright © 2023 by Parent Ready, Inc.

Parent Ready supports the right to free expression and the value of copyright. The purpose of copyright is to encourage the creation of works that enrich our culture.

All rights reserved. No part of this book may be reprinted or reproduced in any form or by any electronic, mechanical, or other means, now known or hereafter invented, including photocopying, recording, and information storage and retrieval, without the prior written permission of the publisher, except in the case of brief quotations embodied in critical articles and reviews.

First Parent Ready trade paperback edition June 2022

Parent Ready and design are trademarks of Parent Ready, Inc.

Bulk purchase special discounts are available. Please make inquiries via https://teenmentalhealth.guide.

Interior design by Kathleen Dyson

Library of Congress Cataloging in Publication record has been applied for.

ISBN: 979-8-9856685-5-1 (paperback)
ISBN: 979-8-9856685-4-4 (ebook)

Contents

Introduction ... 1

Part 1: What Is Normal? ... 3
Chapter 1   Adolescent Development ... 5
Chapter 2   Within the Range of "Normal" ... 7
Chapter 3   What Is a Mental Health Disorder? ... 11

Part 2: Identifying the Problem ... 15
Chapter 4   How Do You Know There Is a Problem? ... 17
Chapter 5   Red Flag Behaviors ... 19
Chapter 6   Gathering Information ... 23
Chapter 7   Talking to Your Teen ... 27
Chapter 8   Responding to Your Teen ... 33
Chapter 9   The Decision to Seek Help ... 37

Part 3: Finding the Right Help ... 39
Chapter 10   Who to Look For ... 41
Chapter 11   Where to Look ... 47
Chapter 12   How to Decide ... 51
Chapter 13   Making the Appointment ... 55

Part 4: The First Visit ... 61
Chapter 14   Preparation ... 63
Chapter 15   To Attend or Not to Attend? ... 69

Chapter 16	The Ride to the Office	73
Chapter 17	In the Office	75
Chapter 18	After the Visit	79
Chapter 19	Processing Information	83
Chapter 20	Knowing Whether the Match Is Right or Not	87
Chapter 21	What If It's Not the Right Match?	91

Part 5: The Diagnosis — 93

Chapter 22	Making the Diagnosis	95
Chapter 23	Discussing the Diagnosis with the Therapist	99
Chapter 24	How Is Your Teen Dealing with the News?	103
Chapter 25	What Does This Mean for the Immediate Family?	105
Chapter 26	Who Do You Tell Outside of the Immediate Family?	109

Part 6: Supporting Your Teen — 111

Chapter 27	Are You and Your Spouse on the Same Page?	113
Chapter 28	What Does Support Look Like?	117
Chapter 29	Dual Diagnoses	121
Chapter 30	Medication Management	125
Chapter 31	Consistent Appointments	129
Chapter 32	Changing the Physical Environment	131
Chapter 33	Chronic versus Acute Diagnoses	133
Chapter 34	Fluctuations in Therapy	135
Chapter 35	Knowing That Things Are Getting Better	139

Glossary	141
About the Author	145

This book is dedicated to my family, for their love and tireless support of everything that I do.
To my mentors, for taking a chance on me and sharing their wisdom. To my cousin Brian, who always saw my light but had his taken away too soon.
And, most importantly, to my husband Glen and two children, Tryston and Zoë, who inspire me every day.

Introduction

When our children are in danger, our natural fight or flight response kicks in. A mental health crisis can trigger this response, opening the gates to a wide range of emotional responses that might leave you paralyzed with fear, isolated, and worried that you aren't doing enough to support your child. Yet being scared is natural, and being worried is normal. It's what we do *after* we acknowledge these feelings that will either set our teen up for success or leave them* struggling to find their way.

Mental health challenges are often seen as mysterious, taboo aspects of life that people hope never affect them or their loved ones. In truth, the World Health Organization reports that globally, one in seven youths, aged 10 to 19, experience a mental health disorder every year. Yet results from the 2016 National Survey of Children's Health show that only 50 percent actually receive treatment in the United States. So, although teen mental health is not often discussed freely, know that you are not alone in this experience. And, in reading this book, I hope that you feel empowered to **_actively_ support your teen** rather than passively endure the challenges associated with a mental health crisis.

I have designed this book to guide you step by step through the mental health process, from identifying behaviors of concern all the way to determining when things are getting better after engaging in therapy. Reading it cover to cover will provide the most comprehensive

---
* The pronoun *they/them* is used in its singular form throughout the book because it is the most practical and inclusive approach.

overview of how to navigate the process, as well as give you the confidence and courage to be the best advocate for your teen. However, you can also read specific chapters to help with areas of immediate concern.

I have been treating adolescents for more than 14 years and, while a difficult road may lay ahead of you, *Navigating Teen Mental Health* will help you shift from crisis-mode to a positive, sustainable, long-term approach that will promote your teen's well-being.

PART 1
What Is Normal?

CHAPTER 1
Adolescent Development

Adolescence is an important period in our lives that is marked by physiological changes, cultural milestones, significant cognitive development, and fluctuations in mood. This transitional period is generally thought to shape the trajectory of adulthood, putting pressure on parents and teens alike to get it right. But what does it mean to "get it right?" The answer to that question is different for all of us, which makes it even harder for parents and teens to create a strategy for success. If you are anything like me, knowing basic facts helps to create a baseline from which I can make logical decisions and/or make sense out of events that occur. Understanding adolescent brain development and how it may influence teens' mental health can go a long way towards giving us the confidence we need to support our teens should a mental health crisis arise.

For example, a parent has noticed that their teen is extremely disorganized, has difficulty getting assignments in on time, their room is a mess, and their mood seems to fluctuate with the wind. Without a basic understanding about adolescent development, the parent may think that her child is lazy, unmotivated, or some other negative adjective. However, if we arm the parent with the knowledge that the teen brain is still "under construction" and that regions of the brain that control higher order thinking and organization don't finish developing until the early 20s, she may stop thinking of these behaviors as character flaws and provide more support to help her teen develop strategies to improve organizational skills.

Additionally, if the parent understands that the emotion center of her teen's brain has more influence on decision-making than what is experienced in adulthood, she can then make the connection that the irrational or illogical decisions that her teen is making are not due to stupidity but instead highly influenced by their emotional state, which fluctuates rapidly when placed in challenging situations.

Adolescent development is complex but at the core of it all we just need to recognize two things. First, every behavior our teen displays is not associated with a negative character flaw that will follow them for the rest of their lives. Often these behaviors are modifiable and a perfect opportunity for parents to provide guidance and support. Second, many of the behaviors teens display fall within a range of normal development and should not be labeled as pathological because they are different from what we experience as parents. Teens are both a part of us and individual beings who will take chances, make mistakes, and evolve into their own unique people if we let them.

CHAPTER 2

Within the Range of "Normal"

Buying into the common stereotype that teens are sullen, emotionally distant, isolated, prone to engage in risky behavior, or untrustworthy can negatively impact parent-teen relationships. When we expect the worst of our teens, we devalue their individuality and put them in a position where no matter what they do they cannot win. From time to time, teens will experiment, try new things, and push the limits of what we, as adults, may think of as "normal" or even safe. Just like adults, teens will also go through emotional ups and downs. Their increased propensity towards risk-taking and this wave of emotion are magnified during adolescence by physiological and developmental changes. Giving teens the space to make mistakes, to develop their own personalities, and expand their mindset can be hard for parents because we think we can anticipate what pitfalls or challenges lie ahead. Logically we know this is a superhuman ability that we do not possess but it does not stop some of us from trying. So we struggle to find a good balance between how much to intervene and how much to leave them to their own devices.

This is definitely the case when dealing with mental health challenges. As parents, it is difficult for us to deal with this unsteady state of emotion because we are typically on the other side of those emotions, trying to figure out the whats and the whys of it. More specifically, when our teens display what we consider to be negative emotions, our protective mode is activated. In the moment, our minds are trying to process questions like, "what just happened?" "is this something my teen needs support with?" or "how can I fix what's wrong?" As hard as it may be for us to witness our teen grapple with the everyday challenges of life, allowing them to handle these emotions to the best of their abilities will support their emotional development and hone their emotion regulation skills—a key component to success in adulthood.

There may be times when the challenges our teens face are so overwhelming that they need more than just parental support. Times when they need the help of a professional with expertise in adolescent mental health. I often get asked by parents, "how do I know when my child needs more than just my support?" My answer is, "pay attention to their behaviors, not just their emotions."

Behavioral Indicators

Let's take a moment to compare how behavioral indicators may manifest in a healthy teen versus a teen who might be experiencing a mental health challenge.

When we envision the behavior of a teen who is following a normal developmental pattern, we may think of a teen who is academically able to keep up, who is doing what is asked of them, who is following societal norms, perhaps challenging them and questioning them, but for the most part who fits in with everyday society and is aware of, and perhaps even focused on, doing the right things within their particular environment. They will pursue activities that are important to them and look for opportunities to engage in those activities. A typical teen will also value friendships and be able to maintain them. They will seek out occasions to spend time with their peers outside of school or extracurricular activities. They will be interactive with family members, connecting with siblings and parents, maybe looking to family members for support and guidance, and engaging in—even looking forward to!—family activities. A healthy teen will keep up with their daily habits, spending time on their appearance, eating regularly, and maintaining a relatively consistent sleeping pattern.

QUESTIONS TO ASK YOURSELVES:

- Is my teen able to connect socially with friends?
- Are they spending time outside of the home?
- Are they focused and excited about events and activities that are happening in their life?
- Are they preparing for their future?
- Are there drastic changes in their behavior?
- Are they eating more or less than before?
- Are they sleeping more or less than before?
- Have their grooming habits changed?
- Are they provoking fights or getting into arguments more than usual?
- Have they changed their friend group?
- Are they using drugs or drinking alcohol?

When we start to think about behaviors of a teen who might be experiencing a mental health challenge, we envision a much different picture. We might imagine a teen who is anxious or worried about going to school, to the point where they procrastinate in the morning, are constantly late, or develop stomachaches or headaches that prevent them from attending school. We might imagine a teen who is irritable, who becomes tearful out of the blue and is not sure why they are crying, who questions life and their worth, who is persistently sad, who refuses to engage in activities, who has difficulty making decisions, who stops brushing their teeth or combing their hair, who sleeps every chance they get, and who barely eats throughout the day. Or a teen who does not have many friends, finds it hard to make friends, or is sad and isolates at home or in their room because they feel like they don't fit in. A teen who has a very negative or cynical outlook on life and/or is easily frustrated, argumentative, and physically or verbally combative could be experiencing a mental health challenge. We can also think about a teen who has difficulty paying attention in class, is fidgety during lectures, constantly forgets assignments or tasks they are asked to do, starts multiple projects at once without finishing any of them, has difficulty waiting their turn, or blurts things out during class discussions. Finally, we can imagine a teen who fights against authority figures, who may start to steal from family members, who does not follow rules, who may be using drugs or alcohol regularly, and who has increased incidents of getting into trouble at school or with the law.

It is unlikely that one teen will exhibit all of the symptoms outlined above. However, when a teen exhibits a few of these behaviors for a prolonged period of time, and when these behaviors start to interfere with their ability to successfully complete daily tasks or engage in social interactions, the behaviors become cautionary flags indicating that the teen may need professional help.

CHAPTER 3

What Is a Mental Health Disorder?

Understanding terms associated with mental health can be a challenge. First, they are not often defined and second, they are often used interchangeably in everyday conversation, negating the nuanced differences that exist between terms. Additionally, when mental health conditions are discussed in the media, symptoms are often exaggerated or depicted at their extreme, perpetuating negative stereotypes. In order for you to truly benefit from this guide, it is important for several terms to be identified and discussed.

The Diagnostic and Statistical Manual of Mental Disorders, Fifth Edition (DSM-V) is the manual that is used by your health care provider to determine the appropriate mental health diagnosis based on your teen's reported symptoms. It contains a list of approximately 297 disorders. Symptoms associated with each disorder and the criteria needed to qualify for the disorder are outlined in detail. Further discussion is included to highlight research findings that may provide context for diagnostic findings and that should be considered during the assessment process. This manual should not be considered the be-all and end-all to the diagnostic process but it serves as a guide for clinicians as they attempt to develop an accurate understanding of what is going on with your teen.

Although your first inclination may be to run out and buy the manual for yourself to forgo the hassle of trying to find a professional, it is important to note that without the clinical expertise needed to use the manual effectively you could do more harm than good. Clinicians spend thousands of hours in training, perfecting clinical judgment and learning to synthesize information from various sources to determine a diagnosis. Honing diagnostic skill is more than just reading text—it comes from experience. However, understanding what the DSM-V is and how it is used by clinicians assures parents that diagnoses are not being derived out of thin air. Armed with this knowledge, parents can ask questions, generating conversation that will help the family feel more at ease with the process.

A **mental health disorder** is described by the DSM-V as "a syndrome characterized by clinically significant disturbance in an individual's cognition, emotion regulation, or behavior that reflects a dysfunction in the psychological, biological, or developmental processes underlying mental functioning. Mental disorders are usually associated with significant distress or disability in social, occupational, or other important activities." In layperson's terms, it is an emotional, cognitive, or behavioral disturbance that impairs a teen's ability to function successfully. This impairment must be persistent as opposed to a unique event. It is common for a mental health disorder to also be described as a *mental illness* or a *mental health condition*.

Often parents feel as though they are alone when they are faced with a mental health condition that affects their teen. You are not alone! Research suggests that nearly one in seven youths aged 10–19 will experience a mental health disorder. Common mental health disorders that are found in teens include social phobia, generalized anxiety, depression, attention deficit hyperactivity disorder (ADHD), post-traumatic stress disorder (PTSD) brought on from abuse or witnessing a tragedy, substance abuse, learning disabilities, and eating disorders. Left untreated, mental health disorders can lead to extreme behaviors that can increase teen mortality. Suicide, which is often linked to severe depression, is the fourth leading cause of death in youth aged 15–19.

Functional impairment is the inability to successfully navigate activities of daily living. For a teen, these activities may include hygiene rituals, attending school, completing homework, developing appropriate relationships, maintaining adequate nutrition, and obtaining adequate sleep. Impairment in one or several of these areas that persists over time is a key indicator of the presence of a mental disorder.

We all have days where we might not be functioning at our best. Occasional instances of poor hygiene or lackluster performances on the field are not cause for alarm. Teens are human and will experience reduced motivation from time to time. Understanding that functional impairment, as it relates to mental health, requires a prolonged period of diminished activity or drastic changes in behavior can help put your teen's behavior in perspective.

Although there will be other technical terms that will be discussed throughout this guide, understanding these three terms in particular is integral to the discussions presented in subsequent chapters. Please refer to the glossary for additional terms.

PART 2
Identifying the Problem

CHAPTER 4

How Do You Know There Is a Problem?

We are often highly attuned to our teen's behaviors. We may think of the quirks and tendencies that they display on a daily basis as character traits that make them uniquely our teen. But there may come a time when we ask ourselves when certain characteristics or behaviors are attributable to "normal" adolescence and when their quirks are a symptom of a clinically significant problem. The short answer is when their behaviors begin to negatively impact their ability to complete daily activities or function in ways that are developmentally appropriate for their chronological age.

When a teen is in crisis it is easier to determine that professional help is needed. For example, if the teen is actively suicidal or displaying self-injurious behavior at home or in school, we instinctively know that this behavior is of concern and spring into action. In these types of crisis situations, schools are more likely to provide an extra layer of support and guidance, such as immediate therapist referrals and/or extra monitoring throughout the day, particularly if the behavior has been displayed on school grounds. Family members and friends who are privy to the crisis are likely to be more understanding, bolstering parent resolve to seek the help the teen needs. The crisis is the point at which parents cannot ignore what is happening and they have difficulty attributing what's happening to a particular incident or some other insignificant excuse.

The more subtle signs that a teen is developing or suffering from a mental health condition can be difficult for a parent to judge. For instance, if the teen is isolating themselves in their room, we may be grappling with whether to give them their independence or be concerned that something is wrong. Or, if a teen starts to appear sullen and unmotivated, we may think that they are just being moody or lazy rather than attributing these behaviors to a depressive episode. These subtle signs do not engender the same panic we might feel in a crisis situation and, because they are less obvious, they do not spark the same types of support from school, friends, or family. This is one of the primary reasons mental health conditions go undetected in teens. As parents, it is important for us to recognize that persistent changes in our teens' behavior that result in **their inability to complete common tasks,** such as finishing their homework, or **interact in ways they used to**, such as engaging with friends, are also indicative of a mental health condition. See the next chapter for more specifics in identifying these subtle signs.

CHAPTER 5

Red Flag Behaviors

The following are common behaviors that are cause for concern and may indicate that your teen is suffering from a mental health disorder. It is important to note that both the presence and duration of these symptoms should be used as determining factors. If these symptoms occur infrequently, we would not consider them cause for concern. However, if these symptoms persist for two weeks or more, and are deviations from how the teen behaved previously, professional help should be sought.

Sleep

Sleep is a key marker of well-being and is particularly sensitive to changes in mental health. Conditions like insomnia, restless leg syndrome, and nightmares are often considered symptoms of, or contributors to, mental health conditions such as generalized anxiety, depression, attention deficit hyperactivity disorder (ADHD), and posttraumatic stress disorder (PTSD). If a parent notices that their teen finds it difficult to fall asleep, stay asleep, or perhaps wakes up extremely early in the morning despite desiring to sleep longer, this could be related to an anxiety disorder. Frequent nightmares or fitful sleep could be associated with PTSD. Sleeping more than usual and being fatigued throughout the day could be linked to depression.

Sleep is a reliable indicator of mental health and enduring noticeable changes that impact daily function should serve as red flags to parents.

Eating Habits

Changes in eating habits are another key indicator that your teen may be experiencing a mental health challenge. Generally speaking, we all follow a consistent eating pattern throughout the day, with either two to three big meals—breakfast, lunch, and dinner—or grazing throughout the day. There may be instances when we are engrossed in an activity and accidently skip a meal or when we are at an event with amazing food and we overeat. However, on a day-to-day basis our eating habits and our appetite are aligned with daily cues and are consistent.

When a teen experiences a mental health challenge it is common for drastic changes within their appetite or eating habits to occur. Teens may eat more when they are depressed as a way of self-soothing or to distract themselves from the negative thoughts they are experiencing. Or they may restrict their eating when experiencing anxiety related to how they are perceived by the world in an attempt to feel better about their looks. Their appetite might be diminished if they are overwhelmed by stress. Paying attention to teen eating behaviors and noticing patterns of food refusal can help parents identify whether a problem exists. Drastic fluctuations in weight can also highlight a persistent pattern of restrictive or indulgent behaviors associated with eating. Be mindful that during adolescence your teen may experience a growth spurt, when their appetite may increase to meet the physiological demands of maturation. However, this growth spurt is very different from a significant increase in weight due to overeating.

Physical Appearance

During adolescence physical appearance is often an important part of our teen's identity. Whether they spend hours in front of a mirror flexing and primping or they carefully cultivate clothes for an "I don't care look," their appearance is integral to the outward expression of who they are. When mental health challenges arise, a teen's motivation or interest in their appearance may diminish. A teen experiencing depression may be less inclined to take showers, brush their teeth, or comb their hair. A self-proclaimed fashionista may not care about their clothes anymore and instead reach for drab sweats. A teen dealing with anxiety may bite their nails to the quick or spend hours in front of the mirror, causing them to be late for school while trying to get every hair in place. A teen struggling with emotion regulation may resort to self-injurious behavior and wear sweatshirts or pants in hot weather to cover up scars. For example, the teen may start cutting themselves to relieve mental pain by focusing on physical pain. Cutting can leave scars or bruises usually in places that can be covered, such as forearms or thighs. Finally, a teen suffering from anorexia may develop brittle hair and soft nails as a result of lost nutrients. Using changes in physical appearance as a barometer of teen mental health can be extremely helpful to parents in knowing when to reach out for help.

CHAPTER 6

Gathering Information

Once you have identified a behavior, or behaviors, of concern it is time to gather more information. This process should not resemble a scene from a murder mystery where you are looking for clues around every corner with your magnifying glass. This should be a short period of time, perhaps a day or two, when you consult with your spouse, connect with the school if appropriate, and possibly talk to other close family members who spend a lot of time around your teen. This process is the first of two steps towards putting context to the behaviors of concern.

Connecting with Your Spouse or Co-Parent

Let's acknowledge that household structure varies from family to family. With that said, connecting with your spouse or co-parent may be a logical first step. If you have the luxury of being able to share your concern with your spouse or co-parent, and you think they will be supportive of your teen, start there. This early collaboration is ideal because it will allow the two of you to level-set and share perspectives. Using this as a starting point ensures that neither parent is left in the dark and it sets the stage for finding a solution together. If one parent is in the dark about concerning behaviors, there is room to misinterpret the behaviors and for them to assign negative attributes to your teen. For example, if your spouse notices that your teen is neglecting daily chores they may think of your teen as being lazy. However, once you provide the other concerning behaviors that you have noticed in your teen, such as isolating themselves in their room, irritability, and declining grades, the neglect of daily routines that your spouse has noticed becomes a piece of a larger picture that points towards depression. Each of us has a unique perspective of our teen that is colored by our own past history, knowledge about our teen, and expectations we may have. As a result, we may focus on different aspects of our teen or interpret their behaviors differently. Discussing our perspectives with our spouse or co-parent allows us to create a clearer picture, adding more context to the behaviors of concern.

Another reason to join forces with your spouse or co-parent at this point is to develop a united front in order to build confidence in your ability to tackle what may lie ahead. Supporting a teen with a mental health condition can be taxing on families, particularly if family members are at odds over the teen's care. Connecting in the early stages, when the behaviors are first noticed, can help to build a more supportive environment and greater understanding of why decisions are being made. One caveat to consider as you move forward is that the united front can become divisive if presented as parents versus teen. Try to keep in mind that the united front is meant to be inclusive of your teen and to build each other up throughout this process. Discuss your feelings with each other, check in with one another, but remember that your teen is not the enemy or the broken child that needs to be fixed. The teen is a critical member of the team and should be treated as such.

Connecting with School

Given that most teens spend the majority of their day in school, teachers can be an excellent source of information regarding your teen's behaviors. If the school has not contacted you first, it is worth sending an email or making a phone call to specific teachers to ask how your teen is doing in class or if they have noticed any changes in your teen's behavior that is of note. A teacher of a subject with which your teen is struggling academically is a good place to start. At this point you do not have to dwell on the issue if they tell you that your teen seems fine. It is possible that your teen does not display any behaviors that raise a red flag for a teacher. For example, symptoms of internalizing disorders, such as anxiety and depression, often go without recognition at school because they are not disruptive to the classroom environment. However, symptoms of conduct disorder, such as verbal combativeness or extreme bullying, can interfere with the teacher's ability to teach the class and are therefore identified more readily.

If the teacher has noticed behavioral changes, ask them to elaborate to help you understand whether there is any pattern to the behaviors. Do these behaviors occur in the early part of the day, only in one class, in a particular classroom environment, or are they limited to less structured parts of the day when there is more peer interaction? The conversation should be less of an interrogation and more of a fact-finding mission.

Connecting with Friends and Family

Friends or family members that your teen is close with can also be extremely helpful during this investigative phase. Often teens will confide in them when they get stressed or start to feel overwhelmed. While we wish they would always confide in us, as their parents, it is perfectly natural for them to build a support network outside of us. This network may include siblings, aunts, uncles, grandparents, cousins, and friends from various places. It is hard to know everyone they may be close to but at least connecting with one or two other confidants in your teen's life could shed more light on the behaviors of concern.

Let's say your teen experienced an interpersonal conflict at school, or within their friend group, that they know their aunt has also experienced. This may be an instance when your teen discloses information to their aunt instead of you. Whatever the teen's reason for tapping into their network of support, it is worthwhile for you to connect with that network to see what they might share. Again, do not be alarmed if the people you talk with do not have any information or if they are unwilling to share details. They may be protecting the boundaries of their relationship with your teen and it means that it is time to check in with your teen directly.

CHAPTER 7

Talking to Your Teen

Broaching sensitive topics with our teens can be difficult. During these moments we are typically trying to walk a fine line between stating some hard truths and not hurting our teen's feelings. Connecting with your teen to discuss behaviors that you have observed, and concerns that you may have around their mental health, falls into this category. Although there may not be a perfect time to have these discussions, there are times that are far better than others. Timing, approach, and preparation are the keys to creating the optimal environment for initiating sensitive conversations about mental health with your teen.

Timing

Timing is a critically important component to setting the stage for a positive conversation. When initiating a sensitive conversation, you want to make sure that you have a designated time and a space that is convenient for both you and your teen. You are thinking, *does such a place exist? And why do I have to go through such lengths to have a conversation with my teen?* This tactic does take more time and discretion on our part, but it will absolutely increase the odds that the conversation that you are about to initiate will go smoothly. Here are three things to consider when choosing the right time to have a conversation with your teen:

1. Do not start a sensitive conversation while your teen is in the middle of something or when you are multitasking. Whether they are immersed in homework, a FaceTime call, or their favorite video game, interrupting active engagement in another activity immediately puts the teen in a defensive posture. If you initiate a conversation while you are cooking dinner, answering emails, or helping a sibling with homework, you will appear distracted, effectively minimizing the importance of the conversation. Try to choose a time on the weekend, when perhaps you can carve out time to go for a walk or take your teen out to dinner. Creating a non-threatening environment, free from distractions, is the goal.

2. Take an open approach to the conversation. Try to let go of the preconceived ideas that you have surrounding the behaviors you have noticed and what you think your teen's response to the conversation will be. Start with open-ended questions and allow your teen to give their perspective on whatever behaviors you have observed. For example, if you notice your teen withdrawing and not interacting with the family, instead of being accusatory and saying, "why aren't you hanging out with the family?" or "you don't spend time with us anymore," you could take a softer approach similar to: "I've noticed that you have been spending more time in your room. How is school going?" Notice that this approach names the behavior of concern and provides an open-ended question for the teen to respond to. When possible, avoid questions that only elicit yes or no responses, as teens may not elaborate beyond the short response. Giving a specific topic to focus on is helpful, as

broad questions can be overwhelming and lend themselves to responses such as "fine" or "okay." With the more refined question you can follow up with specific areas of concern that fall within that topic.

3. Prepare for the conversation. You do not need to have notes in front of you but have an idea of your specific concerns and examples of behaviors or instances that may support your concerns. The royal "we" and phrases like "you always" or "you never" can be off-putting and lessen the impact of your statements so try to avoid them.

REAL-LIFE EXAMPLE

A 15-year-old disclosed that her parents got really mad at her for not coming out of her room when her extended family came to visit. When the teen was asked why she felt the need to retreat to her room, the teen stated that when she tries to spend time with the family she gets peppered with questions laced with judgement. The aunts and uncles would ask questions like, "why are your grades so bad?" or "why do you look like you put on weight?" She stated that it was all very negative. The teen felt as though she was caught between a rock and a hard place. On one hand, she did not want to be disrespectful to her elders. On the other hand, she did not feel as though she should have to subject herself to the negativity on a regular basis. The teen felt vulnerable because she did not have permission to discuss or combat the negative comments and her parents were not sticking up for her. So her solution was to remain in her room. This is an example of why it is important for parents to allow their teens to provide context to concerning behaviors. Without this conversation, the parents might have assumed the worst of their teen. Making sure that we speak with our teen to give them the opportunity to discuss their feelings in a judgement-free zone will help to build the open relationship with our teen that most of us crave.

Potential Open-ended Questions:

- I know this has been a tough year; how is school going?
- Tell me about your hardest subject. What can I do to help?
- Who are you hanging out with at school these days? How is [insert friend's name here]?
- You seem tired lately; what has been keeping you up at night?
- Interesting song choice; what do you relate to most in this song?
- How are you feeling today?
- What activities are you looking forward to this week? (If they respond with "nothing," start to ask about specific classes or activities that you are aware of.)

If Your Child Comes to You

If your child feels safe enough to reach out to you when they are in the midst of a mental health challenge, the worst two responses you can give are apathy and inaction. Stigma around mental health has ingrained the idea that conditions like depression or anxiety are under the teen's control and therefore something they need to "push through." Many parents will treat it like it is "just a phase" and leave the teen to their own devices. It takes a lot of courage for a teen to share their struggles and we need to be cognizant of this fact. When your teen comes to you for help, make time for them—do not brush them off. Putting it off until later may result in the teen shutting down and shutting you out.

Give them the space to talk to you uninterrupted. Save your comments or words of wisdom until you are sure that your teen has said all that they need to say. Be aware of facial expressions that you may make. Your teen will be hypersensitive to criticism and will be looking to see if you are giving negative nonverbal cues. Encourage them to expand the conversation with statements and questions like, "tell me about that," "what does that feel like for you?" or "what are you experiencing?" During this conversation, your goal is to gather as much information as possible so that you and your teen can make a plan. If you feel as though they are a harm to themselves or to someone else, seek professional help immediately by going to the emergency room, urgent care center, or calling the National Suicide Prevention Lifeline (1-800-273-8255). Your actions in this moment can be the difference between life and death.

ACTION ITEMS

- Accept the information that your child is providing.
- Determine whether your teen is a danger to themself or others and requires immediate care. If so, seek help immediately.

In Summary: Clarify the Underlying Concern

What happens if you notice a dramatic change of behavior in your teen?

1. Try to make note of the exact behaviors that are concerning you.

2. Check in with your spouse or co-parent to see if they have noticed similar changes or have similar concerns.

3. Connect with the teen's school and close friends and family for more information.

4. Approach your teen to see if they can provide context for the behaviors, or if they can articulate current issues or problems that they may be experiencing.

5. Seek professional help if the behaviors you have identified are persistent and impair your teen's ability to function.

CHAPTER 8

Responding to Your Teen

Having sensitive conversations with your teen takes courage on both sides. As your teen begins to open up, they will move into a place of vulnerability, where every facial expression, body gesture, and vocalization will be magnified. Being open-minded and willing to listen is very important. But your reaction to what is being said is just as important. Interruptions—words that criticize, pass judgement, or even encourage—can stop the flow of conversation. When the flow of conversation is paused, it can actually cause the teen to shut down or become more selective about the facts that they share. Your goal is to try to minimize your outward reaction to the conversation. Do not check out, but do not react as though you are commiserating with your best friend. Patience is key. Stay interested, truly listen, try to mentally catalogue the key points of the discussion, and save your comments until your teen finishes their thought. Give your teen the chance to fully tell their story.

Once your teen has said all that they need to say, take a moment to think about your response instead of giving a knee-jerk emotional response. At this point, you have to use what you know about your child. Some may need a hug, some may be waiting for your response, and some may just need you to sit beside them for a moment in silence as you both process what they have said. You can acknowledge how difficult it must have been for them to share their story or even thank them for being so honest with you. Let them know that you heard what they had to say. Ask questions about things that were unclear. You want to be supportive and reduce the urge to try and "fix it" in that moment. You can ask your teen if they can identify specific ways that you can support them. If they cannot articulate what they need, share potential ways you might provide support and discuss ideas for moving forward. For example, if your teen is feeling stressed and overwhelmed, you might offer to help them create a manageable plan for making up missed assignments or completing tasks. Your support may include offering to talk to teachers in classes that they are struggling with, to come up with a team plan. It is important for you to take the conversation seriously and to act with urgency, as opposed to waiting for their symptoms to pass. It usually takes a lot for a teen to share their feelings and you need to respect that.

In the event that your teen has shared a story that requires immediate intervention, such as active suicidal thoughts, an assault, or other forms of trauma, you need to gently share with your teen the fact that you will need to seek medical help or police intervention immediately. For example, if your teen says that they wish that they were dead, or that they would be better off dead, you need to feel a sense of urgency with that statement. Do not blow it off as meaningless. When teens are severely depressed, they may feel worthless or like the world no longer has meaning. These types of depressive thoughts increase the risk of suicidal ideation and suicidal attempts. If your teen has been assaulted, this should be perceived as a serious offense that requires police intervention. Seeking help from medical professionals or the police can be scary, but the goal is to keep your teen safe. Assure your teen that you will be with them every step of the way.

A Side Note

As a society, we don't treat mental health conditions in the same way that we treat physical conditions. Often when we notice a symptom of a mental health condition in our teen we brush it off as insignificant or something that will fix itself in time. When we notice a physical ailment, like a persistent stomachache, we will race to urgent care or call for an appointment with our primary care physician as soon as possible. Why is there such a mismatch in responses, despite the negative impact both can have on our teen? As parents, we need to reframe our mindset around mental health to allow us to seek professional help, to treat mental health conditions as we would a physical condition. If we know that our teen is experiencing a mental health challenge, we need to move with urgency to support them without hesitation.

CHAPTER 9
The Decision to Seek Help

Now that you have determined that there is a problem, added context to your observations, and had a conversation with your teen, what do you do next? The toughest decision that a parent is faced with at this point is whether to seek professional help or whether to try and deal with what their teen is experiencing on their own. There are instances when honing time-management skills may help anxiety and increasing quality time with family and friends or engaging in positive activities can prevent isolation and help reduce symptoms of depression. But more often than not, if you have identified persistent behaviors that impair your teen's ability to function on a daily basis, professional help is warranted. Ask yourself:

- Are the symptoms, signs, and behaviors that I have identified keeping my teen from being successful at school?

- Are they keeping my teen from spending time with their friends or family?

- Are they keeping my teen from being able to perform athletically or on stage?

If the answer is yes to any of these questions, it is time to seek professional help.

Life-Changing Events

Life-changing events, such as moving to a new place, divorce, injury, exposure to a traumatic event, or the death of a loved one, could also be reasons to seek professional help. Events of this nature do not automatically result in psychological challenges in teens, but they may serve as precursors to the development of psychopathology. Note that it is part of normal human development for teens to experience a variety of emotions related to these life-changing events. Most will experience sadness at the loss of social networks as a result of a move, for example. Many will feel overwhelmed as they contend with the divorce of their parents. Some may become hypervigilant right after experiencing a traumatic event. All of these responses fall within the range of "normal." However, prolonged responses to events that turn into maladaptive behaviors are a cause for concern and clear indicators that professional help is needed.

Family History

A final consideration that may help a parent discern whether to seek professional help is whether there is a family history of mental health challenges that are similar to what your teen is experiencing. Many types of psychopathology have a heritable component, meaning that genes that are associated with a particular disorder can be handed down to us from our relatives. Having this heritable trait does not mean that it is inevitable that our teen will express a particular type of psychopathology, but it does increase the odds. Understanding the mental health history of your family is just as important as understanding the medical history of your family. This piece of knowledge can help you to know what to look for and spur you into action early to prevent the development of severe conditions.

PART 3
Finding the Right Help

CHAPTER 10

Who to Look For

There are many different types of professionals who provide mental health services, but we know that not all providers are created equal. Providers can be differentiated by the level of training, specialization, therapeutic context, theoretical orientation, and personal characteristics. One of the most important qualities to look for when choosing a mental health provider is licensure. A licensed clinician is subject to review every year or two with regard to their knowledge base and their clinical expertise. Licensure is a way of indicating that someone has passed specific knowledge standards and is competent to provide adequate levels of treatment. Identifying a licensed clinician may also be important for insurance reasons, because most insurance companies will only cover payment for licensed providers. Licensed clinicians can come from multiple clinical fields and will vary in the level of training they have completed. This broad variation in licensed providers expands the availability of therapeutic services but can be confusing to parents as they try to figure out the right direction for their families.

Below we will discuss the most common types of providers and the typical services they provide. Please note that these descriptions are broad overviews or generalizations about each professional category. There will be providers that fit these descriptions perfectly and others that may take a more eclectic approach to their practice and include services that are typical of other provider categories.

Clinical Psychologists

A clinical psychologist is a doctorate-level clinician that has received didactic and clinical training covering the overall field of psychology. They are typically rooted in a specific theoretical orientation, such as cognitive behavioral or psychoanalytic psychology (see glossary for definitions of terms here and below), which helps to shape their patient conceptualizations and treatment strategies. There is often a focus on using empirically supported treatments and identifying measurable outcomes. They can provide clinical, psychoeducational, and neuropsychological assessments in addition to group, marital, family, and individual psychotherapy. Most will specialize in a particular population or context, such as child and adolescent psychology, pediatric psychology, or school psychology. Some will be purely clinically focused while other will have expertise in both the clinical and research realms. Their credentials will include PhD or PsyD.

How they can help: Clinical psychologists cover the gamut of psychological disorders, including severe mental illness. They can provide a wide range of assessments to address behavioral and mental health challenges. They are also the only professional trained to conduct neuropsychological evaluations. Clinical psychologists provide formal diagnoses and conduct non-medicinal treatments.

Important considerations: Finding a clinical psychologist who is accepting patients can be difficult, due to high demand and limited professionals in certain areas. Session rates may also be higher than other non-medical providers, given their level of expertise. Clinical psychologists do not prescribe medication or provide wraparound services to secure additional resources.

Psychiatrists

Psychiatrists are also doctoral-level providers. A psychiatrist has completed extensive training in the medical field as a whole and then specialized in the field of psychiatry during their residency and fellowship years. Like psychologists, they are typically rooted in a specific theoretical orientation, such as behavioral or psychoanalytic theory, which helps to shape their patient conceptualizations and treatment strategies. Their primary focus is on medicinal therapies that either complement psychotherapy or serve as stand-alone treatments. They typically provide clinical and medication assessments with follow-up to ensure proper management. Some will also engage in psychotherapy. Most will specialize in specific areas, such as addiction medicine or child and adolescent psychiatry, but they are almost always found in private practice or hospital-like settings. Their credentials will include MD or DO, with board certifications in their specialty areas.

How they can help: Psychiatrists cover the entire spectrum of psychological disorders, including severe mental illness. They provide clinical assessments to address behavioral and mental health challenges that your teen may experience. They are the only mental health professionals that can prescribe psychotropic medications independently. Psychiatrists provide formal diagnoses and typically provide medicinal treatments.

Important considerations: Finding a psychiatrist who is child/adolescent-focused and who is accepting patients can be difficult due to high demand and limited professionals in certain areas. Session rates may also be higher than all other mental health providers, given their level of expertise and focus on medication management. Psychiatrists do not conduct neuropsychiatric evaluations or provide wraparound services to secure additional resources.

Social Workers

Social workers are either at the master's level or doctorate level. Their approach typically divides the focus between the behaviors and thoughts that a teen presents and the external factors that might be impinging upon the teen's ability to function. In other words, they assess daily living needs and other factors that impinge on the teen's ability to succeed. For example, if a teen is experiencing food insecurity, a social worker will find resources to ensure that the teen has a consistent food source while supporting their mental health needs. A licensed clinical social worker often uses evidence-based manualized treatments that might span multiple theoretical orientations based on client need. Social workers are located in hospitals, schools, private practice, clinics, and community-based settings. Their credentials can include a PhD, DSW, LICSW, or LGSW. LGSW-level clinicians require supervision from a LICSW but are credentialed to practice with some independence.

How they can help: Social work professionals cover the majority of mental health conditions but do not typically focus on treating severe mental illness. They provide clinical assessments to address behavioral and mental challenges that your teen may experience. They are the professionals most likely to assess and support resource challenges that may be impacting your teen's mental health. They can help secure wraparound services to provide additional resources. Social work professionals provide formal diagnoses, secure wraparound services, and conduct non-medicinal treatments.

Important considerations: Most social work professionals are master's-level clinicians with a more focused area of expertise. This type of provider is commonly found in school-based settings or community-based facilities. Social work professionals do not conduct neuropsychological evaluations or prescribe medication.

Licensed Professional Counselors

Licensed professional counselors are typically master's-level clinicians. Their focus is often on the overall wellness of individuals in specific contexts, such as in school counseling or addiction counseling. They will have both didactic and clinical training, with more emphasis on supervised experiential learning. Their theoretical orientation is usually less eclectic than social work and they are more likely to use non-traditional therapies, such as art therapy, in addition to traditional therapies. Licensed professional counselors can be found in hospitals, clinics, private practices, schools, and community-based organizations.

How they can help: Licensed professional counselors typically cover milder psychological conditions. They provide clinical assessments to address behavioral and mental health challenges that your teen may experience. They often specialize in supportive or talk therapies. Licensed professional counselors provide formal diagnoses and conduct non-medicinal treatments.

Important considerations: Licensed professional counselors are master's-level clinicians with a more focused area of expertise. This type of provider is commonly found in school-based settings or private practice. Licensed professional counselors do not conduct neuropsychological evaluations, provide wraparound services, or prescribe medication.

CHAPTER 11

Where to Look

Identifying a mental health provider can be daunting. As mentioned in the previous chapter, there are many different kinds of providers, and there are so many different ways and places to identify help that it can feel overwhelming when you are likely in a heightened emotional state yourself. Setting expectations from the outset can be helpful and potentially reduce the frustration you may feel as you go through this process. Know that there is a shortage of mental health professionals, which means it is unlikely that you will be able to schedule an appointment for the next day. Many providers have full caseloads with wait lists that are months long. If your teen is in crisis and needs immediate attention, the emergency room is the quickest answer. Utilizing the emergency room in a crisis situation will give your teen access to both medical and psychiatric resources to help stabilize them in the moment and provide referrals upon discharge. However, if your teen is not in crisis and you have time to explore alternatives, the following options are available:

Word-of-mouth can identify a provider through friends, family members, or trusted individuals by asking where they may have sought help in the past or if they have a personal connection in the mental health profession. These types of referrals can provide a modicum of comfort because they are endorsed by people you respect and feel safe.

Warm hand-offs from trusted health care professionals, such as your teen's primary care provider or pediatrician, can be helpful because they often come with personal connections that can increase access and expedite scheduling. Health care professionals with whom you have interacted previously and who know your family dynamics could be a really good referral source because they can help you determine the best type of mental health care professional to meet your current needs. For example, if you go to your teen's pediatrician and describe the behaviors of concern, they could direct you towards a mental health professional that can provide therapy based on your teen's needs. If your primary care doctor or the pediatrician are not viable options for referrals, you can also find help within the hospital system that your family receives services from. A children's hospital system, for example, typically has many different departments that could provide mental health services. Look for departments of psychiatry or psychology and inquire whether they have an outpatient mental health clinic with openings or individual professionals who might be taking new patients.

Another safe source for identifying mental health providers is **your teen's school**. Asking the school for a referral is another way to potentially tap into school resources as well as connect with outside resources. Most schools have mental health professionals on staff who can provide services to your teen on site, during school hours. Recently, there has been a renewed effort to expand traditional services within schools by hiring additional providers and collaborating with community organizations that offer mental health services. School staff can also provide community-based resources that might be a good fit for your teen.

Your insurance company serves as a strong resource to identify a mental health professional that is licensed and covered under your current policy. It has a list of professionals that fit various criteria and can identify providers that are within specific distances from your home so that you are not traveling hours for service. The beauty of going through your insurance company is that you can tailor your request to fit personal criteria, such as a female or male therapist or one who specializes in LGBTQ+ concerns. There are also insurance companies that will make the initial appointment for you and provide your insurance information to the professional with whom you will be working. On the downside, it can be difficult to reach an actual person within your insurance company and this process can be a bit time-consuming. However, if you can tap into this resource, it may be most helpful in the long run.

Finally, a less personal yet viable way to identify mental health providers is through **an internet search**. Many professional societies, universities, and hospitals post their mental health clinicians on their websites. Providers who are in private practice are often listed online or have their own websites. The World Wide Web can serve as a valuable resource if you know what you are looking for. The biggest plus for using the internet is that you have everything at your fingertips. You can identify people who are in other states or who are right next door. You can read about the provider's practice and patient reviews. However, this wealth of information can also feel like a barrier to finding help because there is just so much out there. How do you know what is going to be most helpful? How can you identify someone who would be within your network? How can you identify someone who would be the most helpful for your teen's current needs? So if you choose to find help via the internet, understand that there may be more information than you need. Starting with a small number of identified providers and contacting them directly is a good way to start.

ACTION ITEM

Compile a list of all the potential therapists you have identified through the methods provided in this chapter. Your list may only contain five people, or 20. At this point, I'm not asking you to narrow it down or to even focus on the list. Just list the names of the people who could potentially work with your teen.

CHAPTER 12

How to Decide

Ideally, at this point you have identified a list of 10 to 20 providers that might serve as good options for your teen. Unfortunately, due to the aforementioned provider shortages, you may instead have three to five options in your general area. Finding a provider to help your teen is not a "one size fits all" type of process. Licensure qualifications and the current needs of your teen are the most important factors that go into choosing someone to help. However, other characteristics, such as specialty, theoretical orientation (more on this below), race/ethnicity, gender, practice location, and practice hours, are intangibles that can impact treatment. Identifying provider characteristics that are important to you and knowing what's important to your teen from the outset can help reduce the stress. For example, studies have shown that a match between therapist and client race/ethnicity is associated with greater patient satisfaction and positive treatment outcomes, so some may seek out providers who are similar to them with regard to race/ethnicity. Others may favor a particular gender or someone who is LGBTQ+ friendly. Finding a provider that captures characteristics that are important to you and your teen does not guarantee competence or a perfect match, but it does increase the likelihood of establishing an important therapeutic bond.

    You might be asking yourself, "how do I know what characteristics are important to me and my teen?" To answer that question,

I encourage you to think about trusted friends or family members who you are close to and try to pinpoint positive qualities that they share. Think about people you often gravitate to in social settings or even perhaps the makeup of social groups that you belong to. Write down the positive characteristics that you connect with to create a provider wish list.

Also think about the importance of the practice location—are there areas that are too far to travel to or have a lot of traffic, making it difficult to reach an appointment on time? Write those locations on your list as places to avoid. Think about when you will be able to get your teen to their sessions—are there time constraints that you have to consider? Including these preferences on your wish list will not only help you narrow down your options but will also help increase your provider satisfaction in the long run.

Ask Questions!

Another way to help you identify an appropriate provider is to call their office and ask questions. Ask about the provider's theoretical orientation. For example, are they someone who focuses on cognitive behavioral techniques? This means that they assess the antecedents and consequences of a teen's thoughts and actions to devise treatment plans aimed at modifying thoughts and actions that impair your teen's ability to function.

You can ask if the provider has experience working with teens. Although they share the same licensure credentials, adult-focused clinicians may have limited to no clinical and didactic training focused on children and adolescents. As a result, they may employ treatment strategies that are not developmentally appropriate for youth. In addition, some people are more comfortable working with teens than others, allowing them to build a better rapport that often leads to a more open therapeutic environment.

Another important question to consider is whether the provider has expertise in dealing with the symptoms or behaviors that you have identified in your teen. Although their practice may include patients with various disorders, most clinicians have specialty areas, such as anxiety, depression, sleep, or autism. Discerning whether a particular provider has experience with, or expertise in, an area that fits with your teen's symptoms will improve the odds of successful treatment. Let's say your child is having difficulty coming out or understanding their sexuality. Finding a therapist who specializes in LGBTQ+ issues is important, because they will be able to bring to bear aspects of being LGBTQ+ that perhaps another therapist may not be able to include within the therapeutic process. If your teen is experiencing depressive symptoms, it may not be imperative to have someone who specializes in depression specifically, but you will need a provider who has had experience working with teens with depression. This is important because teens express their depression differently than adults. Anger/irritability is the primary symptom for teens who might be experiencing depression compared to persistent low mood and tearfulness in adults. So if you tell an adult-focused provider who doesn't have experience working with teens that your teen is experiencing extreme irritability and has a low frustration tolerance, that provider may misdiagnose your teen with conduct disorder or intermittent explosive disorder because their symptoms do not align with the typical adult manifestation of depression.

Finally, you can inquire about logistics. How often does your provider typically see patients? Are the sessions in person or virtual? Will your teen see the same provider each visit? By asking these questions, you will set your mind at ease and hopefully help your teen feel more comfortable with the process.

In Summary

Collaborating with your co-parent and teen to devise a wish list of provider characteristics and asking questions up front will help you narrow down your list of options and increase your odds of finding a good therapeutic match for your teen. However, it is important to be flexible during this process because is it unlikely that one person will meet all the characteristics on your wish list. Try to be open-minded and use your wish list as a guide. It is possible that the perfect match for your teen may not check all the boxes on your list.

> **ACTION ITEMS:**
>
> 1. Identify providers in your area who work with teens and create a contact list.
> 2. Create a wish list of provider characteristics.
> 3. Call providers and ask questions before making your final decision.

CHAPTER 13

Making the Appointment

Making that first appointment can be a little nerve-wracking but this step is important, given that it opens the door to the therapeutic process. There are three components to this step:

1. Preparing for the call
2. Choosing the best method of contact
3. Making the appointment

Preparing for the Call

Before you schedule the appointment, I recommend having a family discussion with your teen and co-parent. Discuss the next steps, any scheduling conflicts to be aware of, and dates that work best for you all. Be sure to write these down so that you can refer to the list during the call. Be aware of holidays or dates when your family may have scheduled events so that you do not double book. Highlight days off or early dismissals from school, as they may increase your teen's availability.

Choosing a Method of Contact

There are lots of options when it comes to connecting with providers: the old-fashioned office call, the "contact us" sheet that many websites have, or an email to the provider or practice. I recommend calling the practice directly because it allows you to ask questions and schedule all in the same call. One caveat: calling can be a little frustrating because you may be sent to voicemail or, due to high demand, you may be on hold for a long time. Try to be patient and remind yourself that you are calling for a good reason. Hopefully, after the wait and your discussion with the practice you will leave the phone conversation feeling more comfortable and confident that you are making the right decision. If you make the phone call and something just seems off about the practice or the practitioner your teen will be working with, trust your instincts and move on to another provider on your contact list. That initial phone interaction can give you important information about the practice. Make note about how the administrator or provider treated you on the phone. Think about the ease and speed of service you received. These aspects of the practice can help guide your decision as to whether this is a practice that you would like to continue with.

If email is the only way of connecting with your mental health care provider, you can simply ask if they have any openings available or let them know that you would like to schedule an appointment for your teen. You do not have to provide a detailed account of your concerns, but a brief description is helpful because it gives the provider an opportunity to prepare for the session in advance. You also give them the opportunity to let you know whether the services they provide are appropriate for the needs of your teen, instead of coming in for a session and feeling as though you wasted your time if it is not a good match.

Finally, you can schedule an appointment through the practice's website. Many web portals have a "contact us" page, which is an electronic form that will request basic information, allowing an administrator to respond to your scheduling request. Forms of this kind may ask questions regarding your teen's symptoms or may strictly focus on basic contact information. The disadvantage of using this method, like with email, is potentially not receiving a response in a timely fashion—or at all. If you do not get a response within three to five days, you should follow up using a different method of contact.

Scheduling the Appointment

When you are scheduling the appointment by phone, be sure to have the lists you prepared in front of you. These include the important dates and times, the contact list, your wish list of provider characteristics, and any questions that you want to ask. It is also helpful to have paper and pen nearby so that you can take notes during the call. Begin by asking if the provider is taking new patients and takes your insurance. By starting with these questions, you will reduce the number of times you have to tell your story. Once the practice is established as a possibility, you want to ask your questions before scheduling the appointment. Once you are satisfied with the responses, use the date and time list to help you find a date that works for the provider and your teen. It can make for a difficult first session if your teen is annoyed because you pull them out of class during a major test or make them miss an important activity they wanted to participate in to take them to therapy. Try to coordinate family schedules to the best of your ability to avoid negative first impressions. Sometimes you do not have the luxury of finding a mutually agreeable time with the provider. In that instance, try to pick an appointment date and time that is the least disruptive to your teen's schedule. A similar effort should be made to accommodate your schedule, to avoid a frantic race to the office and being late to the appointment.

The Dreaded Wait List

Winding up on a wait list can be frustrating and disappointing. Unfortunately, there is a shortage of health care professionals that focus on behavioral health in certain areas of the country. A wait list is used when a provider has a full caseload and is currently not accepting new patients. In theory, the wait list keeps patients on the provider's radar for when there is a spot available in their practice. Sometimes a wait list can extend out a month or two, which can be difficult for parents when they perceive that their teen is in an immediate state of crisis. Remember, if it is a true urgent situation, call 911 and seek care through the emergency room or visit an urgent care center. These services exist to provide the help your teen needs in the moment and then can provide referrals for outpatient or longer-term care.

If your teen is not an immediate danger to themselves, then temporary services from a school provider or their pediatrician can potentially offer some tips or tools to help your teen deal with mental health concerns as you patiently wait for an appointment. Even as you wait to get an appointment with your first choice, try the other providers on your list to see if your teen can get an earlier appointment in another practice. You can always cancel if you end up with two appointments. If that happens, try to notify the practice as soon as possible so that another teen in need can have your spot. Sometimes there are cancellations and providers can fit you in earlier than what they initially projected on the phone. It may not be an ideal time, but try to be flexible and accept the appointment if possible. The first few appointments are critical to the assessment process and may take longer than subsequent appointments. Once you are added to the provider's caseload, it can be easier to make follow-up appointments.

ACTION ITEM

Never give up! Continue to search and contact therapists for as long as it takes. There will be a provider available for your teen, whether through telehealth or in person; you just have to be persistent.

PART 4
The First Visit

CHAPTER 14

Preparation

Now that you have scheduled your teen's appointment, it is time for you to prepare for the actual visit. Whether the date is just around the corner or three months away, there are things you can do to foster a positive experience.

First and foremost, make it a point to check in with your teen regularly. This does not mean continuously asking, "How are you feeling today?" as that can get old and, without any real method of changing things in the moment, teens can view it as a pointless question. Instead, inquire about specifics around their day. For example, "How was math class today?" or "What did you talk about in science today?" or "How is [insert friend's name here]?" These pointed questions allow for teens to begin a dialogue with you that could lead to other topics. By starting small conversations, you also create moments to observe behavioral indicators that show how they may be functioning that day. If your teen is isolating themselves, try to encourage or arrange more opportunities to share space with them. You do not have to attempt to engage them constantly, but think of ways to simply be in the same room with them. Perhaps you set up a work space for them in the living room or prepare a family meal where everyone eats together. You can invite them to watch a show with you or even run errands.

Checking in with your teen while you wait for the appointment will also help you keep tabs on whether the severity of the situation has changed. If you find that your attempts to check in are exacerbating your teen's symptoms or causing conflict, pull back and just monitor from a distance. As long as your teen's safety is not in jeopardy, you can afford to give your teen a little space until their appointment date. This does not mean becoming totally hands-off and relaxing family structures that already exist. It just means that if they cannot answer your questions, or prefer to spend time alone, you do not have to push the issue.

A Week Out

As you get closer to the appointment date, approximately a week out, connect with your teen and co-parent to assess everyone's comfort level surrounding the impending appointment. Ask your teen how they are feeling about the upcoming appointment. Some teens will have asked to see the therapist because they know they need someone to talk to, or they know that it can be helpful, so they are raring to go. But that's not the majority of teens. Other teens are ambivalent about whether or not they should go. They may know something is wrong, or that they need help, but they are not quite comfortable with the idea of going to the therapist, given all the stigma that is attached to it. So having a conversation about their worries, their fears, and their expectations can help set the stage for a more productive session. If you know your teen's concerns up front, you can talk to the provider ahead of time to let them know that your teen might be feeling a certain way, or that there might be something that your teen might want to address at the beginning of their session. Some teens may not be inclined to discuss their feelings in this moment and that is okay. Checking in and giving them the opportunity to discuss their worries ahead of the session is your goal. Do not make this conversation a point of contention.

Gather questions that were discussed about the process, or the provider, so that you can bring them to the appointment. Often, we think when we go to a provider that they have all the answers and we are just there to listen and let them ask questions of us. It is important for you and your teen to feel comfortable when you are in that therapeutic room. To promote that comfort, you should be prepared to ask questions about things you are unsure of, whether it be about the process, the therapist's technique, the length of therapy, or whether or not therapy is even needed. These are all great questions to ask when you go into that first session. I suggest writing them down in advance, because once you get in the provider's room, your focus on and worry about your teen may cause you to forget your questions. On the other hand, you all may not have any questions at this time, which is alright too. However, uncertainty about the process may be causing anxiety and this would be the perfect time to acknowledge it.

Day-of Plan

During your family meeting you can also discuss a "day-of plan," which will help you iron out the logistics. There are times when families rush into my office, frazzled because their efforts to get there on time turned chaotic. This, in turn, put the teen in a surly mood or caused them to be preoccupied with the challenges they faced en route. A "day-of plan" will help clarify logistical assumptions and allow everyone to be on the same page. For instance, discuss whether your teen will need to miss school or whether a parent will need to take off from work or leave early. Identify who is picking up your teen for the appointment, as well as a specific pick-up time and place. Be sure to leave an extra time cushion before and after the appointment to account for traffic, changes in schedule, and unforeseen events.

On the back end, therapy and assessments can run longer than anticipated from time to time. Typically, we try to keep sessions within a one- to two-hour window, depending on the type of assessment or therapy that is needed. However, there are times when we may run over, for example, if you have additional questions or if we feel like there is additional information, such as details about a particular incident, that we need to gather before the session ends. By adding a cushion to the back end of the session you will feel less overwhelmed if the session runs long.

It is also important to determine who will be attending the session with your teen. It is advantageous for both parents to attend the first session, but that is not always feasible. Come to an agreement as to who will attend with an understanding that if only one parent attends, they will include the concerns/observations/questions expressed by the other parent.

Finally, discuss whether you all would like to plan an after-visit activity or just go straight home. It may seem odd to think about, but an after-visit activity can help all of you process the therapeutic experience in a non-threatening way. So you could go out to dinner or get a special treat to provide a safe place for your family to regroup and discuss next steps.

Staying Organized

My final recommendation is to gather all the behavioral observations, feedback from teachers and family members, and your list of questions in one place. Some parents put it all in a folder or binder to help keep things organized. Academic items such as testing, reports, or teacher feedback can be helpful. Documents that outline any pertinent medical history may also be useful, such as previous mental health encounters as well as diagnosed medical conditions.

Observations that you made as you identified the behaviors of concern, and any patterns that you noticed surrounding those behaviors, are helpful. For example, you may have noticed that your teen gets irritable when they come home from school—that it usually takes them two hours to start their homework and they don't always complete it. This simple observation can be helpful to your therapist. New behaviors or events, changes in habits, or traumatic experiences will also be valuable information for your provider.

Keep in mind that your provider is not likely to take the file or notebook you create and read through it page by page. However, organizing your information in this format can help you be prepared to answer questions they may have during the initial assessment. Depending on the information, some providers may ask to keep a photocopy of the information for the teen's records. In other cases, your verbal report of the information will suffice.

> **ACTION ITEM**
>
> Don't feel like you have to have every detail written down. Take your time, think about the day of the appointment, and decide what's best to include for you and your family.

CHAPTER 15

To Attend or Not to Attend?

This is a big question for parents: "Should we show up or should we stay home and allow our teen to have some independence?" As parents, we are often walking a fine line between doing what we can to protect our children and giving them space to develop the competence they need to be successful in the world. In this situation, it's important to show as much support as you possibly can. My advice is to attend the very first session. You may make other decisions down the line, but the first session is a really important one because it lays the groundwork for building a therapeutic alliance.

If possible, both parents should attend the first session. This is important because we all see things through a different lens; what one parent sees, the co-parent may see differently. It is also likely that a teen has a different relationship with each of their parents, which may lead to additional insights for the therapist. Having both parents in the first session increases the probability that everyone is comfortable and on board with the therapeutic process. Therapy can become stressful when parents disagree with the provider's approach or second guess the process. If neither parent can attend, having another supportive adult attend with your teen is a good substitute. I have had occasions where grandparents accompanied the teen to their sessions because a parent could not get off work.

Your teen may be ambivalent about your presence at the first session or may flat out tell you not to come for a variety of reasons. This is a moment where you do not have to ask their opinion. Simply let them know you will be attending. By attending this first session, you acknowledge the importance of therapy and show support for your teen all in one action. It shows your teen that you are committed to finding them the help that they need. This situation might be compared to when they are competing in a sporting event, when they land a role in the school play, or when they have a band recital. They do not always ask us to come but we show up anyway to support them. Having that support, whether it's asked for or not, means a lot to your teen. Please note that showing up does not mean taking over the session or even participating in the session at all, depending on provider preference. It does mean showing up prepared to support your teen as appropriate, even if that means you play a minimal role.

Another reason I recommend that parents attend the first session is because, despite what your teen may think, you have an abundance of information about them. Providing historical context to the challenges your teen is currently facing is valuable information for your teen's provider. We often ask parents at the start of the session if they have any concerns that we should be aware of. At the end of the session, we will ask if there is any other information that the family thinks may be helpful. Both questions are perfect opportunities for parents to share helpful insights. Try not to be long-winded in your response. Share the insights that are pertinent to your concerns. If your teen's provider needs more detail, they will ask additional questions.

Attending the first session can also put your mind at ease. It can be a disconcerting feeling to know that your child is talking to a stranger about their problems and potentially about your family.

So checking out the practice environment and experiencing the provider's demeanor firsthand can help you establish a basic level of comfort that you will need if or when you send your teen into the office unattended. Small things, such as how the provider greeted you and your teen or the therapeutic environment's chaos level, are important. And how your teen behaves in the moment can provide invaluable data points that will impact your comfort level and help you decide whether you want your teen to move forward with this particular provider.

> **ACTION ITEM**
>
> Discuss who will attend the first session with your co-parent and come prepared (see chapter 14).

CHAPTER 16

The Ride to the Office

The ride to the office can be as normal as we would like it to be. In the movies this scene might be depicted by a teen and a parent sharing an awkward silence or an irritable teen in the corner, looking out of the window, and a parent who is detached in the moment. But in truth, this ride is similar to the many rides you have taken before, just like when you have taken your teen to the doctor's or dentist's office. The ride to your first session should be as typical as you can possibly make it. So if you normally listen to music while you are in the car with your teen, do so. Do not feel like you have to have a full-on conversation with your teen in that moment. If you are normally chatty with them about their day, go for it. It can be a great opportunity to check in with them. Try to avoid "hot button" topics that may lead to conflict or put them in a negative frame of mind as they walk into the office.

Whatever the challenges that your teen currently faces, please keep in mind that this is a positive step. You may celebrate their courage after the session, but on the ride there take comfort in the fact that it should be thought of as an ordinary appointment. If your teen is exhibiting behaviors that lead you to believe they might be anxious, you have three easy options:

1. Talk to them about it.

2. Try distraction techniques to refocus their thoughts on positive things.

3. Remind them to practice relaxation techniques that work for them.

Often when we are faced with the unknown, repetitive negative thoughts about what may happen fill our minds and can spiral into catastrophic thinking—a state of mind where it feels as though everything is going terribly wrong. Your teen may be worried that they will say all the wrong things or that the therapist will hate them. If you perceive that your teen is anxious, you can distract them from repetitive negative thoughts by engaging them in conversation that requires more than just yes or no answers. For example, ask them what they are excited about regarding an upcoming trip or maybe discuss a TV show you all watch together. If your teen has already mastered a relaxation strategy, like taking deep breaths while counting to 10, suggest they engage in that technique. Or even play some calming music. Refocusing their worries through centering and calming can help them stop ruminating about what negative events *may* happen in therapy.

CHAPTER 17

In the Office

Now that you have made it to the office, what can you expect during your teen's first visit to a mental health provider? One of the first things that your teen's provider should discuss are the limits to confidentiality. Providers prioritize your teen's safety above confidentiality. Under most circumstances, what your teen says in therapy stays in the therapeutic space. However, if your teen ever shares that they plan to harm themselves, someone is harming them, or that they intend to harm someone else, your provider's duty to report is triggered and they must break confidentiality. So rest assured that even though you may not know every detail of what happens in your teen's therapy session, you will know if your child's safety is at risk.

During the visit, be as supportive as possible. If you are invited to participate in the therapy session, try to avoid accusatory or negative language. Discuss your observations and perspective in a way that is not assigning blame or attaching negative attributes to your teen. Remember to state the facts and provide examples of specific behaviors. This is when your notebook or file folder will come in handy. However, let your teen speak for themselves whenever they can. Even though you may know the answer, try to encourage your teen to answer the questions directly. If you let your teen take the lead when you are in the room, it is usually easier for them to continue the conversation when you are not in the room. This approach allows rapport to build between the therapist and the teen while the teen is supported through your presence.

Try to avoid making negative gestures or facial expressions. During the first session your teen is likely to be hypersensitive to perceived criticism. They will be constantly analyzing and thinking about how you react to what they are saying, and how the therapist responds to their answers. Be sensitive to the fact that your teen is hearing the things that you are reporting. Sometimes the things we discuss are really hard for teens to hear, particularly if there has been a trauma and/or a seminal event, such as a death in the family. If there is something sensitive that you wish to privately share with the therapist, you can ask to speak to them without your teen in the room. It is up to the therapist to explain how confidentiality works in these situations and to explain why there might be a need for parents to share information without their teen present. Similarly, if the teen has information that they want to share without their parent in the room, the therapist will usually reserve space for that to occur.

If your teen does not want to talk during the session, that is okay. Keep in mind that you are asking your teen to come into a stranger's office and essentially tell all their private thoughts and emotions. Some teens open up to providers really easily. But the majority of teens are not as comfortable sharing their intimate thoughts or expressing the challenges that they are experiencing with a stranger. So if your teen chooses not to share the details of the challenges they are facing in that first session, do not worry—they are not alone. And it is not a loss. If you have a therapist who is skilled at building rapport, they will understand that a lot is being asked of your teen.

Sometimes parents forget the appointment is not for them and will take over the session by giving too much information or discussing issues that are not related to the behaviors of concern. They want to give as much information as possible, which is helpful, but they end up taking over the session. So really be mindful of the amount and depth of the information you are providing.

What do you do once your teen goes into the session without you? Take some time to yourself and allow yourself to feel content that your teen is in good hands and that they are going through the therapeutic process as they should. If you leave the office, be sure to return at least 15 minutes before the end of your teen's session. Most therapists will want to have a chance to talk with the parent at the end of a session to give a broad overview and to discuss next steps.

CHAPTER 18

After the Visit

The time after the visit can be a little tricky, because your brain may be running a mile a minute and you may be unsure of what to do next. Should you talk to your teen about their session on the car ride home? Or should you sit in awkward silence and give them time to process it on their own? Hopefully, you took some time to create your "day-of plan" as described in chapter 14. Refer to the plan and follow through. If you decided to go straight home, a quick check-in during the car ride home can test the waters and provide your teen an opportunity to share what they are comfortable with. Here are a few potential questions to get your teen talking:

- How are you feeling?
- How did the session go?
- Is there anything that stood out about the session that you wanted to discuss? If yes, what would you like to discuss? If no, what would you have changed about the session?

By asking these types of questions, you are opening the door for conversation. If they choose not to walk through that door and engage, you must respect that decision. If they do share, remember that it is not your job to judge or critique what they are saying. This is a time for listening, unless they ask you a pointed question. Try to end the conversation on a positive note. Praise them for their courage or congratulate them on making it through their first session. Tell them you are proud of them or encourage them in some way. This is helpful because your teen might still be second-guessing therapy and your encouragement will remind them that they are doing the right thing.

If you have an after-visit activity planned, you can use the car ride to decompress before checking in with your teen during the activity. One of the most common activities is grabbing a bite to eat or enjoying your teen's favorite dessert before heading home. Engaging in an activity can help to avoid the awkwardness of just staring at each other. Eating and the comfortable atmosphere of a restaurant might help your teen to relax and feel more open to sharing their thoughts. When choosing where to sit, try to pick a table that affords a little bit of privacy. You do not want to be smack dab in the middle of a restaurant where other people might overhear your conversation and your teen might feel self-conscious. Also try not to pick a space that has loud music playing or an extremely noisy ambiance. Once you have ordered your food you can open the door for conversation and move forward at your teen's pace. Remember to ask basic questions that are open-ended as described above. Your goal is not to get a play-by-play of the session but instead to get a general idea of how your teen felt about the experience. Respect their privacy and do not get offended if they do not give you a lot of information. If your teen redirects the conversation or stays silent, take their cue and let it go. Trying to force your teen to talk could potentially negatively impact your relationship or increase tension.

If your teen did not want to go to therapy from the start, they may reiterate this sentiment and insist that they do not want to go back. Try to be compassionate about their discomfort with therapy, and then try to help them understand that it may take time for them to feel the benefits of their work. Therapy is not a magic pill that works overnight, and it takes time to build rapport with the therapist, so help your teen understand that they will need to be patient and persistent. On the other hand, you might find that your teen had a great session with the provider and is excited to go back. Giving your teen the opportunity to verbalize the fact that they are okay with going to therapy, and that they are happy with their therapist, will also put your mind at ease.

CHAPTER 19

Processing Information

In the previous chapter we discussed strategies to help your teen decompress and process their first experience with a mental health provider. However, it is also important for you to take time to process *your* experience. Many of us like to think that this is just our teen's issue or that it is just another challenge to overcome. In truth, the stress we experience when our teen is in jeopardy is often greater than any other stress we may experience. Processing your concerns and experiences can help relieve your own stress and anxiety. Taking time to process how you feel about the session with a spouse or close confident can help you. Journaling is another way to help you process your experience. As you write, you should consider how you felt during the process; how your teen described their feelings, thoughts, or concerns about next steps; and any additional questions you may have. Often when we go through very emotional experiences, we do not remember the details. Writing things down will help you to track progress over time and help you recall details of the process that you may otherwise forget.

As you sift through the mountain of emotions that you have experienced, you may find that you are still worrying about your teen. This is completely normal. Although you may have found the right path, nothing has been resolved. That fact alone may bring a modicum of comfort, but the reality is that you may still have a long road ahead. At this point it can be helpful to identify and adjust your expectations. Take in the information that the provider shared and try to understand how that fits with your family's goals and your teen's needs. For example, your teen's provider may share an initial diagnosis and a potential long-term treatment plan that you will need to integrate into your family's schedule. Going through this exercise may generate more questions than answers but it will help you organize your thoughts and, in turn, relieve some of your anxiety. You may start to second-guess the therapist's choices, but by discussing or writing down your worries, you have the opportunity to go through them logically and potentially problem-solve to find manageable solutions. I would encourage you not to make any rash decision about therapy at this early stage. Unless the session went horribly wrong, you should give the provider and your teen a few sessions before determining whether it is a good fit.

As much as you'd like your teen to be happy to attend therapy and to feel relieved after the first session, that is not always the case. You may find that your teen is fighting you tooth and nail because they are not ready for therapy. Part of your processing should include thinking about how that first session went for you and your family. Did you and your teen get into a big argument before or after the session? What caused that blowup? Is it something that had to do with therapy itself? Is it something you have worked through? Or is it something that leads you to believe your child needs help in a different way, such as a detox facility? These are all questions that you should think about, process, and write down. Remember, you do not need to have all the answers. These may be topics you bring to the therapist at the next visit, and they can help you wade through them to figure out the best approach. Perhaps you talk it through with your spouse or co-parent. By discussing these topics together, you can consider solutions in the context of what works for your family. You will be the best judge of what your family needs, given your knowledge of family dynamics and other factors that may influence what is happening in the moment. During this process, be confident in that knowledge and use it to make decisions that you think will promote the success of your teen and support your family.

CHAPTER 20

Knowing Whether the Match Is Right or Not

We often say that matching with a therapist is a lot like dating. The first therapist you meet may not be the perfect therapist for you or for your teen. Do not be alarmed if, for some reason, you feel like the provider may not be the right choice. Therapists always value constructive feedback from their patients. If there is something that can be done that might put the patient at ease or that might be helpful for a therapist to know so that they are able to personalize the patient experience in a different way, most providers will adjust. However, there are times where there are mismatches in personality, style, or approach that are irreconcilable.

After the first visit it may be helpful to revisit the provider wish list you created earlier in chapter 12 to determine if this particular provider checks those boxes for you and your teen. If so, that's great! Perhaps there is just a personality quirk that will iron itself out over time. Keep in mind that we are often hypercritical of people when we first meet them, particularly when we are trying to decide whether we can trust them with our teen. This can create a few awkward moments that may not translate into a bad match overall, just first-session dynamics. I would encourage you to attend another session unless something egregious occurs (more on this in chapter 21). Typically, after session two or three we have a better idea of how therapy will go and what type of rapport your teen and their provider have developed. This additional knowledge makes it easier to decide whether the provider is a good match.

A few questions to ask yourself when contemplating whether or not the provider is a good match are:

1. Does your teen feel comfortable?

2. Have you seen your teen smile?

3. Have you seen your teen relax in the environment when the therapist was in the room?

Some teens are just anxious by nature, particularly when they are going into an unknown situation. Even if they are initially anxious, hopefully by the end of the session you saw at least a little reduction in anxiety so that you can tell that they had a good conversation, or that they have made some headway.

Additional things to think about as you decide whether to pivot are:

1. Did the clinician explain things clearly?

2. Did they take the time to talk to you?

These are important questions to ask yourself, particularly in these first sessions because they speak to the provider's approach to working with parents. It is important for the provider to interact with the parents because you are an integral part of the team. Your support, or lack of support, for the teen's care has a strong influence on the treatment's success. It can be hard to go in blindly and just hand your teen over to someone you barely know. A good clinician recognizes this and will have a conversation with you to discuss boundaries that have to be put in place in order for therapy to be a safe space for your teen. They will answer questions that you have to help you feel comfortable with the process. It is clear that teens do not live in a vacuum and that they need their parents' support. You want a clinician who promotes that engagement and who works towards building stronger communication between the teen and the parent, rather than trying to work with the teen independently.

As much as you may focus on your perceptions of the provider and how the session went, your teen's experience is probably the most important consideration. So even if you are not necessarily excited about the therapist because they did not engage with you in the manner that you expected, they might be great with your teenager. Your teen smiling for the first time in a while, or animated conversation, or laughter coming from the therapy room are all really good signs that your teen's provider is doing what they are supposed to do. Yes, you should be aware of *your* feelings about the therapist in the clinical environment, but also pay attention to how *your teen* is feeling about it. In the end you should give greater weight to how your teen is reacting, given that you have limited access to the clinician.

CHAPTER 21

What If It's Not the Right Match?

Identifying another provider and starting all over again can be difficult, particularly if it took a long time to get the appointment in the first place. If you have called, asked your questions, set up an appointment, waited three months to get into the office, and then come to the conclusion that the therapist is not exactly the right match for your teen, that can be extremely frustrating. It is important to understand that it is not unusual to have an imperfect fit with a provider and that it is okay to try to find another one that works better for your teen. Although we want to be careful that we are not making premature decisions to pivot, there are instances where it is necessary. For example, is the provider doing all of the talking and not valuing your input? Or is the provider blaming you or your teen for the current challenges, or using accusatory language? Is the provider snapping at you or your teen? These are clear signs that the provider is not right for your family.

Once you have decided to find another provider, go back to the steps that I outlined in chapter 11. The most efficient route may be to connect with your insurance company again and let them know that the original provider was not a good fit. It can help you get a jump start on finding another provider in your area. Talking to other trusted sources and using some of the other strategies mentioned in chapter 11 are viable options too.

Please note that pivoting in this moment is not a failure. Finding the right match is an important ingredient towards your teen's success. Similarly, keep in mind that if it does not work out the first time, it does not automatically mean that therapy is not for your teen. It just means that you have to find the right provider—and that may take a little bit more time and effort than you initially planned.

The other thing to be mindful of as you go through the process of finding a new therapist is that each time you go to a new provider, you are asking your teen to tell their story again, which can be emotionally charged and/or draining. It is hard for a teen to give of themselves to strangers over and over again. We like to think that our teen is resilient, and they are, but they are also human. Asking them to tell their story or to relive a traumatic moment with multiple therapists may be unfair. If you find yourself in this situation, you may want to revise your initial approach. You and your co-parent can talk with the new provider initially and then bring your teen into the session if you feel there is potential for the relationship to work.

PART 5
The Diagnosis

CHAPTER 22

Making the Diagnosis

After you commit to a provider, they will identify a diagnosis that will guide your teen's treatment plan. It may feel as though the diagnosis that your provider conveys materializes out of thin air—that it is just a subjective label that they created and does not actually mean anything. On some level this statement is correct, as there is a component of subjectivity that goes into a diagnosis. However, the same is true for diagnoses you receive from medical doctors or other health care professionals that focus on physical ailments. By Merriam-Webster's definition, a diagnosis is "the art or act of identifying a disease from its signs and symptoms." This means that your provider will use their expertise to synthesize the signs and symptoms that you and your teen share with them to identify the category of disorder that best explains what your teen is experiencing. They will use symptom criteria backed by scientific evidence to determine whether your teen qualifies for a particular diagnosis. There may be symptoms that overlap with multiple conditions, or symptoms that are attributable to other factors. Your provider's job is to bring clarity to the overlap and to interject their knowledge of how contextual factors impact behavior in order to explain the most appropriate diagnosis for your teen. The science guides the decision-making process, but it is the years of training and clinical experience that help your provider to become adept at accurately diagnosing teens.

Your teen's provider will use the first one to three sessions to assess your teen's mental health. During this assessment process, your teen's provider may employ a variety of different tools in addition to your in-office verbal report and behavioral observations. Your clinician may ask you and your teen to fill out **self-report measures** that will inquire about history and symptoms within specific time frames. These measures allow the provider to compare your answers to those collected from similar respondents. Self-report measures are typically derived through scientific study and help to bring more objective data to the assessment process.

Teacher reports help your provider understand your teen's behavior within various contexts. Teachers spend a lot of time with your teen and therefore serve as vital reporters of your child's abilities and behaviors during school hours, where they spend the majority of their day. Often a provider may ask you to give a self-report measure to your teen's teachers, or they may just ask that teachers provide a summary of their impressions/observations about your teen.

Psychoeducational testing may be used if there is a question about your child's intellectual capabilities or academic achievement. A psychologist will work with your teen, through a battery of cognitive tests, to help identify problems with memory, processing speed, attention, and other areas of intellectual function. Testing of this nature takes multiple hours and might be conducted over multiple sessions. Once complete, a summary report is typically created for parents and can be shared with your teen's school.

Neuropsychological testing is a more comprehensive version of psychoeducational testing, in that psychologists are interested in the brain-behavior connection. Specific areas of function, such as working memory, long-term memory, spatial recognition, and other cognitive processes are evaluated within the context of behavioral function. Neuropsychologists undergo specialized training to develop expertise in this area.

In the next chapter, I outline how to discuss the diagnosis with your therapist.

CHAPTER 23

Discussing the Diagnosis with the Therapist

As discussed in chapter 22, after the first few sessions your provider should provide you with a diagnosis—if one exists. There are times when a teen may be encountering mental health challenges that do not rise to a clinical level and therefore do not qualify for a formal diagnosis. If this occurs, ask your provider for next steps or viable options to help alleviate the concerns that brought you to their office. Depending on these concerns, there are a variety of options that may be available to your teen, and your provider can help direct you. For example, they may refer you to a sleep specialist if your teen is irritable, feels fatigued throughout the day, or snores loudly at night, but does not meet the full criteria for depression.

If your teen does receive a diagnosis, now is the time to ask questions. You can ask the provider questions that pertain to the diagnosis, questions that may pertain to the course of your teen's treatment, or simply inquire about what the diagnosis may mean for your teen. If your teen is diagnosed with a serious mental illness, such as bipolar disorder or schizophrenia, you should ask questions like, "how will this impact our family?" or "what changes might we see as the condition progresses?" Asking questions will help to alleviate the uncertainty or the fear that you might be experiencing. A lot of us feel uncomfortable asking questions in situations where we think that we should know the answer. But in this situation, it's important for you to have as much information as you possibly can. Remember, no question is a dumb question. Ask whatever questions come to mind, and allow your therapist the opportunity to answer them.

Just as important as asking questions is listening to the answers with an open mind. Try not to have a preconceived notion of what your therapist is going to say when you ask your question. Ask the question in a clear and concise manner and then try to hear the response that is given. I acknowledge that hearing something is wrong with your child is not ideal. However, it's important that you listen with an open mind so that you can figure out how to move forward and perhaps how to get your child past the current challenges. If you disagree with something your provider shares, state your concern and discuss it with the provider. Perhaps it is about something that you or your teen reported during their session but the provider misinterpreted. Make sure you discuss this concern with the provider, as the information could have an impact on the overall diagnosis. Do not be afraid to challenge something that you know is incorrect or something that you feel may not be appropriate for your family, such as provider opinions on religion, drug use, and sexual practices. If challenged in a respectful manner, the therapist will understand the questioning and will take the time to discuss the issue.

If you have broached the subject respectfully and the provider does not respond in a way that addresses your concern, that could be a red flag. You want a therapist who can communicate with you as well as your teen. Behavioral characteristics of the provider matter, as they may impact your ability to support your teen as they go through this challenging period.

INTERNET WARNING

It is natural to want to have more information about the diagnosis. You have just been hit with something that can be difficult to process and that may be eliciting a wave of emotions. For some of us, the answer is to rush to the internet to find out as much information as possible. Educating ourselves is always beneficial. However, it is important to understand that not everything that we read on the internet or consume through the media is always accurate. It is true that understanding what your teen is going through can help you navigate the challenges they are experiencing, but if you take on the position that you are an expert because of an hour's worth of internet research, you might be doing yourself more harm than good. It is natural to be curious and to want more information. Just be careful about going down a rabbit hole, trying to uncover everything that has been written about your teen's diagnosis. It can be helpful to do a time-limited search on credible sites, such as nami.org, apa.org, and adaa.org, where you jot down questions that you can bring back to your teen's provider, who will help you sort through conflicting or inaccurate information. Additionally, by working with your teen's therapist to understand the diagnosis, you get further insight into how your provider views the diagnosis within the context of their therapeutic approach.

CHAPTER 24

How Is Your Teen Dealing with the News?

Once a diagnosis is given there is no turning back, no "unhearing" the label. For some, the diagnosis will bring a sense of relief, to finally have a name for what your teen is going through. For others, the diagnosis may increase anxiety and bring an overwhelming dread about what the future holds. You know where you fall along that spectrum, but you can't assume that your teen has landed in the same spot. Check in with your teen to get a better understanding of where they fall and what supports they may need to process the news.

Ask them how they feel about the new diagnosis. In doing so, you want to make sure that they are not blaming themselves for something that was out of their control. Ask them why they feel the way they feel. Do they think that something's wrong with them? Are they worried about what other people may think? Are they relieved to know that there is a name for what they have been experiencing? Do they feel any different now that they know? You can ask a variety of questions to understand their perspective and how they might be feeling about moving forward with treatment.

Try to normalize mental health disorders throughout your conversation. This means making sure that they understand that they are not the only teen who has this condition. Millions of Americans live with mental health conditions and letting your teen know that they are not alone can be comforting. Allow your teen to ask their provider questions about the diagnosis. You will likely find that your teen has a few questions or concerns that are different from yours. But even if their questions are the same as yours, let them voice those questions themselves.

CHAPTER 25

What Does This Mean for the Immediate Family?

When you receive your teen's diagnosis it can feel like your mind is racing in 50 different directions. You might be worried about how this may impact you, your co-parent, and your teen on a personal level. You might be questioning how your family will move forward from this or what it means for the family. I have seen parents blame themselves, feeling as though they had a hand in creating the disorder within their teen, asking if the condition is a result of something they have done, or failed to do. I encourage you not to blame yourself. Look instead for answers on how to resolve the challenge and how to help your teen move forward. Working in collaboration with your teen's provider is the best way to start.

You may also be asking, "now that we know my teen has this disorder, does that mean their siblings will have it too?" Research has shown that mental health conditions can stem from a combination of heritable traits—things that we pass down in our genes—as well as the environment. The environment can encourage the manifestation of different traits that already exist within the individual. For example, a teen may have a family history of depression but never experience a depressive episode. A teen with a similar history may not experience a depressive episode until faced with the sudden, tragic death of a loved one. The development of a mental health condition is never guaranteed, regardless of whether a family history exists. However, family history can increase the risk of certain conditions. So, your teen's sibling may be at an increased risk and the sibling should be monitored if symptoms begin to manifest. Note that if the sibling does not have symptoms, you do not need to take proactive steps towards therapy.

Another one of those 50 questions that might run through your head upon receiving your teen's diagnosis is, "how do we broach the news with our teen's siblings? Should we tell them at all?" This is a family decision that should be discussed with your teen. In an ideal world, bringing siblings into the conversation when they are old enough to understand what it means would strengthen the family unit and provide additional support for your teen. However, in reality, siblings may react in a negative way or become bogged down with worry that may exacerbate the situation. You have to take that into consideration and decide the best approach, with input from your teen. If possible, I recommend sharing the diagnosis with siblings in a way that coincides with their developmental level. This means not going into detail with younger children and defining things more specifically for older siblings. I recommend having the conversation as a family instead of taking the sibling(s) aside and saying, "hey, this is what's happening…" in a secretive manner. Really embracing the idea that therapy is important and that you will work together as a family to get through this challenging time is important. Family unity is conveyed both through words and through actions. It is likely that the sibling is aware of some of the challenges your teen has been going through already. With that in mind, it can be more helpful if they are brought into the fold of supporting your teen versus it being a secretive situation that feeds into stigma that they may have around mental health. If you choose to share the news, be sure to remind the sibling about your teen's right to privacy. Be specific;

discuss potential people and situations that the sibling should not share the information with so that they understand the boundaries of your teen's privacy. Be prepared for them to ask why. This is a natural response for younger children in particular.

ACTION ITEMS

- Ask your teen how they feel about sharing the diagnosis with their sibling(s).
- Share the news as a family unit, with your teen present, to present family unity and support.

CHAPTER 26

Who Do You Tell Outside of the Immediate Family?

Discussing your teen's diagnosis outside of your core family unit is really a personal decision. Some families don't discuss it outside of their immediate core family—those who are living in the home—or a biological parent living outside of the home. Others find it helpful to garner support from extended family members who may have gone through similar situations themselves or who may have a close relationship with your teen.

This goes back to gauging what other family members will do with the information and how supportive they will be of your teen and the family as a whole. You should ask yourself whether telling particular family members puts your teen at risk for negative feedback or being the butt of jokes at the next family dinner. Will they send unsupportive texts or emails to the teen that negatively impact their self-confidence? Will they tell other people who you prefer not to know? Those are important things to consider. While we would like to think that this would never happen, the reality is that many family members perpetuate the stigma around mental health and equate mental health challenges with a lack of resiliency within the teen.

Instagram and TikTok are full of memes in which teens are suggesting that they isolate themselves from family members, and even from their parents at times, because they are tired of hearing negative comments that affect their mental health. There are instances where family members may make comments that seem innocent but the teen takes these personally and internalizes it, making them feel worse about their challenges. So, as you think about who you should discuss your teen's diagnosis with outside of the core family unit, remember to consider how supportive the individual will be throughout your teen's mental health journey.

PART 6

Supporting Your Teen

CHAPTER 27

Are You and Your Spouse on the Same Page?

Given the stigma about mental health, there are occasions when spouses, co-parents, or guardians find themselves with differing beliefs about allowing teens to enter treatment. If your point of view differs from that of your co-parent, you might be asking yourself, "how do I help my co-parent see the value of mental health treatment for our teen?"

Parents come with all types of hopes and dreams about what their teen will grow into as they become an adult. We think about how they will act, what they will do, how successful they may become. When they are facing mental health challenges, we continue to hold expectations that may not align with reality. Our past experiences, coupled with these expectations, may lead to the belief that what the teen is going through is a temporary challenge and they just need to push through it. We may think that they do not need professional help; they will get through this on their own *if they are tough enough*. This "old-school" mindset can have a detrimental effect on your teen. They are not who we are. Society and the context in which they are living is different from what we experienced. And their needs may be different from ours. Their diagnosis does not make them any less of a person, and it is not an indication of poor parenting.

Becoming a parent who is open to mental health services for their teen can be a huge step for some people. This is because emotions, cultural beliefs, and religion are often strong influences on parenting. But the more parents model the importance of mental health, the more likely their teen is to take their treatment seriously and put in the effort to get better. As you embark on this journey with your teen, have discussions with your co-parent about how they are feeling about the process and about their thoughts around mental health. Helping each other to answer questions and deal with potential worries is important. At times we may feel as though we have all of the answers ourselves. But as we start to discuss things with our co-parent, more questions may arise, or more ideas about how you can support your teen as a family may come to light. Ironing out the logistics of supporting the therapeutic process can make this experience easier. Perhaps it is something as simple as coordinating transportation or deciding who is cooking dinner. Whether it be the day-to-day details or the actual treatment plan itself, communicating openly with your co-parent is the ideal situation.

It is no secret that when parents are not in alignment, discord can make any process more challenging. However, there are instances when it feels impossible to get on the same page. If you find yourself in this situation, you should strive to provide a consistent environment for the teen. This may mean not contradicting one another in front of your teen, refraining from sharing negative personal views about your co-parent, and trying to come to a consensus on a path forward, whether it is something both parents believe in or not. Once both parents agree to this particular path, you begin to act as a team. If your co-parent agrees to a treatment approach despite being skeptical about therapy, try to provide updates on the progress that your teen makes. If they continue to have questions, respect their right to parent your teen and involve them to the extent that it is helpful. Getting input from your co-parent may force you to look at things from a different perspective and could be valuable data for your teen's provider. Resolving any potential challenges that your co-parent may bring up will help you feel more confident and comfortable in the decisions that are being made.

Divorced Parents

Divorce can complicate the therapeutic process. The primary issue that I encounter when working with teens of divorced parents who are not in alignment around therapeutic goals is different expectations in different households. For example, if a teen is given a daily homework assignment during therapy to be completed by the next session, one parent might be more supportive by reminding them to complete the daily activity. The other parent, who is not on board with the therapy, may tell the teen, "you don't need to do the activity while you are here"—a statement that completely undermines the therapeutic process.

Doing your best to agree on a therapeutic path, and holding each other accountable for supporting your teen, is the key element to success. If for some reason it is not possible for you and your ex-spouse to work together, alert your provider. When I know a teen is going to a particular household without therapeutic support, I will assign a different activity or perhaps no homework at all. Keeping your teen's provider in the loop can be helpful in navigating situations where one parent is not on board.

I strongly recommend having both parents attend the first session, and any other session that allows both parents to ask questions, so that they can discuss any fears or anxieties that they might be experiencing. Having everyone in the room at the same time increases the chances of getting everyone on the same page, as opposed to one parent relying on third-party information. So, although divorce can seem like an impediment, there are ways that families can work together to provide a nurturing environment for their teen while they are going through therapy.

CHAPTER 28

What Does Support Look Like?

Support is a very broad term that means different things to different people. When it comes to deciding on an optimal method to support your teen, go straight to the source and ask *them* what works best. Your years as their parent may lead you to believe that they like to be left alone, or that they prefer music when they are trying to calm down, or that distracting them with an outside activity would be helpful. Yet asking them directly is the most efficient way to support them in a way that best suits their needs in the moment. You can keep those other ideas in your back pocket. We never forget the things we learn as parents, and they may still come in handy. However, as your teen is maturing, their support needs may be changing.

Check In with Your Teen

Check in with your teen more often. Past history may lead you to believe that you are bothering them or that the check-ins are annoying, but maybe it is what they need right now. Give them a hug. Many parents do not think about hugging their older teens as much as they may have hugged them when they were younger. It's possible that your teen may not even know they need the hug until you offer it. But sometimes a hug is exactly what they need.

Support can look different depending on the teen. It is not a one-size-fits-all proposition. When you ask your teen how you can best support them, you are showing that you are open to their feedback and that what they want matters. This little act can go a long way toward reenforcing the parent-teen bond that may have been impacted by the challenges that the teen is currently experiencing. There is a fine line between overstepping boundaries with incessant questions and checking in periodically. The more that you converse with your teen, the more you will understand what their needs are as you go along.

Check In with the Therapist

The other way to identify strategies that can best support your teen is to talk to your teen's provider. Ask the therapist about other ways to offer support, in addition to what you typically do. They may have some ideas that are specific to your teen's disorder. For example, if your teen suffers from anxiety, the therapist may suggest that you show more patience and help your teen to logically problem-solve when they feel that their anxiety is taking over.

The therapist will likely suggest helping your teen to do their therapeutic homework assignments. Homework assignments can be tough for your teen to complete because they often challenge areas of behavior or thinking that are difficult for your teen. For example, a teen with social phobia may be given a homework assignment to approach a salesclerk to ask for a specific item. This simple act forces a teen with social anxiety to engage in conversation with a stranger who may evaluate them negatively, which is a core fear of teens with this disorder.

Some questions to ask your teen are:

- What homework assignment are you working on today? (See above example.)
- Is there something I can support you with? (You can accompany them to the store.)
- Is there something that you need help with? (Choosing which item to ask for.)

Again, there's a fine line between overstepping boundaries with incessant questions versus periodic check-ins. We often second-guess ourselves. But it's a bit of trial and error. The more you check in and converse with your teen, the more you'll understand what their needs are.

CHAPTER 29

Dual Diagnoses

Managing a mental health disorder on top of a chronic physical health condition may present additional challenges. When the mental health condition develops as a result of the physical condition we call this a dual diagnosis. For example, a teen has an established diagnosis of asthma and has become increasingly frustrated or overwhelmed because they are not able to do the things that they used to do before the asthma diagnosis. Their emotional symptoms may continue to increase over the course of a few weeks, developing into a depressive episode. Or a teen who has just been diagnosed with diabetes might develop anxiety over having to prick their finger every morning in order to monitor their sugar levels. These types of combined physical and mental conditions can be difficult for a teen to manage, particularly when they are first diagnosed.

Rest assured there are ways to manage both diagnoses. Having a physician that is sensitive to the fact that your child also has a mental health condition is important. Notifying the physician that your child is seeing a mental health provider can be an important way to help find a balance between their chronic condition and whatever mental health challenges they're experiencing. Often physicians and mental health providers collaborate to ensure the best treatment approach for your teen. If your teen does not already have a therapist, ask your physician to refer you to one who might be able to help with the mental health challenges that have developed as a result of the chronic condition.

Another type of dual diagnosis is when a second mental health condition develops as a result of an existing mental health condition. For example, a teen that suffers from extreme anxiety to the point that they cannot leave their house may become depressed because they are deprived of social interactions with peers and can no longer participate in activities that they used to enjoy. Or a teen that has post-traumatic stress disorder could develop insomnia in an effort to avoid nightmares related to their trauma. At times it can be hard to determine whether there is truly a second disorder or whether the new symptoms are connected to the original disorder. When new symptoms develop, share them with your teen's provider as soon as possible to better inform the course of treatment.

Co-occurring Diagnoses

It could be that the two conditions your teen is experiencing (either a mental health condition and chronic physical condition or two mental health conditions) have nothing to do with each other. They just coexist but are not connected in the sense that one was created by the other. In this situation, there will be days when one condition may be more challenging and other days when the second condition is more prominent. The goal is to manage both by targeting the symptoms of concern when they flare up and maintaining consistency with the symptoms that are stable. It is important to help your teen find balance in order to successfully navigate living with co-occurring conditions.

It may also be the case that one condition exacerbates symptoms of the other. Let's say a teen has diabetes yet also suffers from OCD. It is possible that the teen becomes obsessive about some aspect of their diabetes regimen, or that a particular food compulsion may impact their sugar levels. In this instance, it is important to discuss the negative interactions between the two conditions with your teen's primary care and mental health providers so that they can tailor the treatment plans accordingly.

Understanding the mind-body connection can help you identify additional challenges that may arise. Mental health conditions like anxiety or depression can have physical symptoms that develop into illnesses, such as ulcers or migraines, if left untreated. So, while it is not necessary for you to diagnose new conditions that may develop, it can be important for you to identify pertinent symptoms and share them with your teen's providers so that they can work together to treat your teen.

CHAPTER 30

Medication Management

There are three effective strategies for treating mental health disorders. The first strategy focuses on the use of various types of therapies, such as cognitive behavioral therapy, supportive therapy, mindfulness, and dialectical behavioral therapy to resolve the presenting problem(s). The second strategy takes a purely medicinal approach, with a focus on introducing psychotropic medication to alleviate mental health symptoms. The third approach combines the first two strategies, such that both medication and therapy are used to treat mental health symptoms. Fortunately, there is empirical evidence that informs providers as to which approach is most effective for various disorders. Your provider will rely on this science, as well as your teen's particular circumstances and symptoms, to decide what strategy might work best. There are many types of providers who can provide therapy, but a psychiatrist would be most qualified to assess whether medication is warranted for your teen's condition.

Although stigma still exists around therapeutic methods for treating mental health conditions, there is even more stigma around medicinal therapies. It does not help that media has often portrayed teens who have received psychotropic medications as unresponsive zombies. So many parents have the misconception that medicating a teen equates to a complete personality change and loss of the child they once knew. This is not the case. Over the years, more attention has been focused on understanding the impact of psychotropic medications on youth with mental health disorders. Instead of being treated like little adults, more recent studies have sought to uncover not only appropriate dosing levels for youth but also how the medications impact developmental trajectories as well as overall function. Medication can be an effective tool to resolve severe mental health symptoms. And for some teens, medication can help take the edge off so that they are able to take advantage of behavioral therapies. For example, if a teen is so anxious that they cannot engage in exposure therapy from the outset or focus on what the therapist is asking them to do, medication can help reduce the symptom expression in the short term so that the teen can engage in therapy that will promote lasting relief.

Another misconception is that medication is an easy fix to prevent behaviors that parents are having a hard time managing. A good psychiatrist will not provide medication just to appease a parent if it is not the best course of action. They will do an assessment and decide whether medication is appropriate for your teen within the context of their presenting symptoms. If medication is deemed the appropriate strategy, they will start your teen off with a small dose and adjust up, until they reach a dose that is effective. Their goal is to find the lowest dosage that provides the most symptom relief. They will not prescribe large amounts of a particular medication to sedate your teen to the point of taking away their endearing personality traits.

Most research shows that medication is not the be-all and end-all. Medication combined with behavioral treatments is the best line of defense for a number of conditions. So being open to medication for your teen is important and finding a provider that you trust to be able to guide you in that journey is also key. Remember to ask questions, such as:

- Why is medication over behavioral treatment the best strategy?
- What would the outcome be if our teen did not take medication versus if they did?
- How long would our teen need to be on the medication?

Variable Medication Schedules

In some cases, your psychiatrist may recommend a medication schedule that varies from the daily consumption we expect. As the provider is assessing your teen, they will consider what behaviors or symptoms need to be managed with medication. They will also ask you to offer context for the behaviors, such as how often they occur and what environments they occur in. Based on that assessment, they will determine if more flexible usage is appropriate. For example, teens being treated for ADHD may take their medications throughout the week and engage in a "medication holiday" on the weekends. Another variable schedule for a teen with ADHD might include taking medication while the teen is in school to manage disruptive behaviors and taking a "medication holiday" when school's out for scheduled breaks.

This approach can decrease concerns for parents who are concerned about their teen using medication. Parents should never make the decision to alter their teen's medication schedule on their own. If your teen's psychiatrist does not recommend an alternate schedule on their own, parents can bring the topic up so that the pros and cons are discussed. Your teen's psychiatrist can disclose the positives and negatives of creating an alternate schedule in the context of your teen's needs. While this type of schedule does work for some teens, others need consistency. So before you stop any medications or make any decisions on your own, please consult your psychiatrist to make sure that this is the right move for your child. The goal is to help your teen function as normally as possible and to alleviate the distressing symptoms that they experience because of their mental health condition. Whichever schedule you and your teen's provider agree to, compliance is key. Maintaining therapeutic levels of the medication in your teen's system can only be achieved through taking them as prescribed by your teen's provider. Parents can support their teen by reminding them, setting up schedules, or setting alarms to help them comply with the treatment regimen.

CHAPTER 31

Consistent Appointments

Keeping consistent appointments with your teen's provider is a key element to successful treatment. Unless your teen is sick or otherwise unavailable, you should help your teen keep consistent appointments with their therapist. The therapist will help direct how often your teen should meet with them to reach the goals of the treatment plan. But regardless of whether daily, weekly, bi-weekly, or monthly appointments are set, consistency is key. In order for the therapy to work, your teen needs to be consistent with the process, which means committing to making the most out of their meetings with their provider.

To be fair, consistency is not always easy. Events will pop up unexpectedly or extracurricular activities may overlap beyond our control. Working with your therapist to reschedule is something that you should do in advance, if possible. Most clinicians try to be flexible. So I would recommend that you give your therapist a call ahead of time, try to schedule your appointments as far in advance as you can, and then make sure that the appointment is on everybody's calendar. That way everybody can be aware of the scheduled time and share responsibility for helping your teen stay consistent with their appointments.

CHAPTER 32

Changing the Physical Environment

Sometimes we unintentionally create spaces in our homes, work spaces, or other environments that contribute to symptoms of our mental illness. For example, if a teen with OCD lives in a house with excessive clutter, that environment can exacerbate compulsions to clean or straighten things up. Providing a living environment that is relatively clean and organized can help the teen feel less anxious. Another example is a teen with major depression who spends most of their day in their bedroom, with limited access to family and friends outside of school and meals. Following the principles of behavioral activation, a simple change in scenery could help improve the teen's depressive symptoms, such as encouraging the teen to complete their homework at the dining room table. Our physical environment can truly impact how we see things and what we do. Making sure that you have ample light in your house can be a small but important factor that influences sleep and mood.

Chaotic, noisy environments have been shown to increase the risk of adverse outcomes in youth. For example, a teen experiencing severe anxiety came into my office with persistent worries across multiple domains of life. In our initial assessment, I discovered that the family kept the TV on news channels all day long because the parents wanted to stay informed. Further discussion with the teen revealed that they felt overwhelmed because "everything seems to be going wrong in the world," and the constant drone of bad news from the TV magnified their fears and worries on a daily basis. A simple remedy was to ask the parents to limit their news consumption to 30 to 60 minutes per day and remove, or limit, the teen's use of social media for a specific period, like a week. After they reached the end of the week, the teen and their parents discussed appropriate limits on social media use moving forward. The teen's anxiety decreased drastically within this first week of intervention.

CHAPTER 33

Chronic versus Acute Diagnoses

If you have a teen who is going through a mental health challenge, and you are taking them to therapy, you might be asking, "how long will this last?" or "will this be forever?" No clinician can answer that exactly. Each teen is different and their response to treatment will vary. Discussing your teen's prognosis with the provider and going over the proposed treatment plan for your teen can help you understand the road ahead. Some providers will collect behavioral response data along the way that they will share to help you see any therapeutic gains or setbacks.

There are treatments that are very goal-directed and can be completed in shorter periods of time. But if your teen has been suffering from a mental health disorder for a long time, you cannot expect that the treatment will be completed overnight. It is possible that a longer treatment regimen that spans a year or more is needed to help your teen recover.

Each teen's response to treatment will vary. Some will respond well to more structured behavioral strategies, while others respond better to the open flow of supportive therapy. Or their response could be influenced by the provider's approach. For example, when targeting phobias through systematic desensitization, the provider may initially choose an anxiety-provoking stimulus that is too uncomfortable. A good clinician will alter their approach based on your teen's response and begin again with a stimulus that falls lower on their fear hierarchy.

There are conditions that are amenable to short-term treatments, such as an acute stress reaction, or an adjustment disorder, which by definition has a defined period of symptom expression. However, conditions such as bipolar disorder or schizophrenia that are connected to changes in the brain may be lifelong conditions that your teen will learn to manage. Conditions like depression or anxiety can be episodic or chronic, which will also impact their treatment trajectory. There will be times when symptoms of the teen's condition will be less impactful on their ability to function and other times when the symptoms will feel overwhelming. Checking in with your teen and communicating with their provider will increase your teen's overall chances for success.

CHAPTER 34

Fluctuations in Therapy

Therapy rarely has a straight trajectory. For some teens, therapy is very effective from the start and, once they feel relief from the symptoms, they discontinue treatment. For others, therapy will show initial success and the teen will see progress and be motivated to continue. After that initial surge of success, though, the progress may slow or stagnate and the family might feel as though therapy does not work anymore. Or the treatment takes longer than expected to show gains and the teen becomes skeptical about the process.

The therapeutic process takes time and is often impacted by things that are going on in a teen's life. For example, when someone is in crisis and the provider works with the teen to help them overcome the crisis, the teen and the family may feel like they do not need therapy anymore. But there is still work to be done to help the teen deal with the underlying factors that led to the crisis in the first place. And that work is much harder, at times, than dealing with the crisis itself. This is because progress can be slow in treatment. This is a point where managing your expectations is critical. Try not to fixate on the day-to-day progress or the speed of your teen's recovery. Think of treatment as you would a long-term investment. The day-to-day could be volatile but as long as the sum gain is in a positive direction you are on the right path. An example of overall positive change is witnessing your teen using therapeutic strategies during challenging moments as opposed to completely shutting down. There will be gains and losses within the therapeutic process, but no specific day can be used as an indicator of success.

What If Therapy Makes My Teen Cry?

If you see that your teen is crying in therapy, do not jump to conclusions. It could be a good thing, a natural part of their healing process. They could be revealing something emotionally impactful or something that they have never told anyone else before. Crying is a natural human reaction when we feel vulnerable. It can be cathartic. Or perhaps the provider is pushing your teen to engage in a therapeutic strategy that is very difficult for them. For example, exposure-based therapies for anxiety require the teen to engage with the very thing that they are anxious about. During this engagement, teens can feel overwhelmed or feel as though the required task is more than what they can do. Your teen may cry and even be reticent to return to therapy because the provider is pushing them to their limit. This is when they need parental support more than ever. Although exposure can be hard for some teens to engage in, it is a technique with strong empirical support. So, in this instance, your teen's provider is not using the technique to hurt your teen, but rather to help them overcome fear that has been impeding their ability to function. Good providers will be understanding and help them get through these tough sessions.

Praise the Positive

Like most of us, your teen will have more success during treatment if they are given a lot of positive feedback and encouragement. Try to highlight improvements in function that you have observed. Particularly with conditions like depression, there is a tendency towards negative thinking that might obscure your teen's ability to see their own successes. Your teen may be focused on all the things that are going badly in their life and will not be able to identify the things that are positive or the improvements that they may have made in therapy. Help your teen to see those positive moments and talk with their provider so that they can also highlight those improvements for you and your teen. For example, if you notice that your teen is making more of an effort to connect with the family, or that they are starting to turn in their missing assignments at school, praise them! Tell them how proud you are of their efforts. Noticing these small changes might not seem that important to you but they will mean a lot to your teen.

CHAPTER 35

Knowing That Things Are Getting Better

How do you know when things are getting better? You are probably looking at every behavior, trying to figure out if your teen is making progress. Have they started brushing their teeth more regularly? Have they started getting out of bed earlier in the day, as opposed to sleeping until 2 p.m.? Are they interacting with family more often? Are previous habits slowly being reintegrated into their daily routine? These are small behavioral indicators that your teen is getting better.

Your teen's responses during your check-in conversations can also provide clues towards their progress. If they are more talkative or providing more in-depth responses, that is a good sign. They may even tell you point blank that they are feeling better. Ask them about some of the strategies from therapy that they think are working. This question is helpful for two reasons. First, you can see how much your teen is retaining skills that are presented by the therapist. Second, you can keep the information in your back pocket to pull out if your teen finds themself back in crisis, or if they forget what they are supposed to do in the heat of a difficult moment. Improvements in their academic function are also a telltale sign. Are they paying more attention to their studies, completing assignments, or able to give presentations? Feedback from your teen's teachers can be another way to determine whether your teen is getting better.

Closing Advice

If the world were a perfect place, there would be a magical moment where our teen just popped right back to who they once were, before the mental health crisis began. But treatment is a slow progression, so acknowledging the positives along the way is going to be important. Give your child the opportunity and flexibility to take the time they need to get better. Continue to check in with your child to ensure their safety. Be cognizant of verbal triggers and people, activities, or events that may negatively impact your teen's mental health. Be open to what the therapeutic process may bring. Feel confident that you have done the right thing by taking your teen to therapy and supporting them throughout this journey.

Glossary

Acute stress reaction — A disorder that occurs after exposure to a traumatic event but lasts less than a month in duration.

Adjustment disorder — A disorder that develops because of a change in a patient's environment, causing maladaptive behaviors.

Attention deficit hyperactivity disorder (ADHD) — A disorder characterized by difficulty with attention, hyperactive behavior, or a combination of the two.

Behavioral activation — A type of cognitive behavioral therapy that teaches patients to engage in positive behaviors to reduce depressive symptoms.

Behavioral theory — A theory that emphasizes the role of behavior in understanding and treating psychological disorders.

Clinical assessments — An assessment strategy that occurs in the office setting and incorporates verbal reports as well as self-report measures completed by the teen and their parents.

Cognitive behavioral therapy — A class of empirically supported treatments that target maladaptive thinking and behaviors.

Conduct disorder	A disorder characterized by a blatant disregard for rules and societal norms. Teens with this disorder may be verbally combative, commit theft, hurt animals, and/or bully peers.
Depression	A disorder characterized by low mood, irritability, and persistent negative thoughts. Teens with this disorder often worry about things that happened in the past and have difficulty identifying positive aspects of the present.
Dialectical behavioral therapy	A type of cognitive behavioral therapy that teaches patients to regulate their emotions, focus on the present, and develop healthy strategies to cope with stress.
Evidenced-based manualized treatments	Treatments that are supported by multiple rigorous research studies, with manuals that provide step-by-step implementation guidance.
Exposure-based therapies	A group of cognitive behavioral therapies that expose patients to anxiety-provoking stimuli in order to help them overcome fears.
Functional impairment	The inability to successfully complete various aspects of daily living as a result of an illness.
Maladaptive thinking and behaviors	False thoughts or behaviors that do not conform to conventional norms or that impair a person's ability to function.
Mental health disorder	An emotional, cognitive, or behavioral disturbance that persistently impairs a person's ability to function successfully.

Mindfulness	A therapeutic technique that teaches patients to focus on the present, while calmly acknowledging and accepting their feelings, thoughts, and bodily sensations.
Neuropsychological assessments	A battery of psychological tests that are used to assess specific areas of function, such as working memory, long-term memory, spatial recognition, and other cognitive processes that are evaluated within the context of behavioral function.
Post-traumatic stress disorder (PTSD)	A disorder that occurs after exposure to a traumatic event with symptoms that have persisted for a month or more following the event.
Psychoanalytic theory	A theory that emphasizes the role of personality development in understanding and treating psychological disorders.
Psychoeducational assessments/testing	A battery of tests that are used to assess a person's intellectual capabilities or academic achievement.
Psychotherapy	A general term that describes psychological treatments that do not include medication.
Self-report measures	Paperwork that a clinician asks a patient (and parent, when appropriate) to fill out that outlines history and symptoms that may have occurred within specific time frames. These measures allow the provider to compare your answers to those collected from similar respondents and are typically backed by scientific research.

Supervised experiential learning	A component of a mental health provider's training in which they conduct therapy under the supervision of an independently licensed clinician.
Supportive therapy	A form of therapy that relies heavily on the therapeutic alliance to help patients meet stated goals.
Systematic de-sensitization	A type of exposure-based therapy that uses a gradual approach to exposing patients to stimuli that cause fear.

About the Author

Dr. **Tyish Hall Brown** is a licensed Clinical Psychologist who has just recently transitioned into the position of Director of Behavioral Sleep Medicine within the Division of Pulmonary & Sleep Medicine at Children's National Hospital.

Before moving to Children's National, Dr. Hall Brown was a tenured Associate Professor and served as the Director of the School Based Behavioral Health Program at Howard University. The HU School-Based Behavioral Health Program was funded by the DC Department of Behavioral Health and strived to support the mental health of youth and their families by seamlessly integrating mental health services into the academic environment. With regard to clinical work, Dr. Hall Brown provided clinical services to children and adolescents using cognitive behavioral techniques to treat conditions such as sleep disorders, anxiety disorders, depression, and attention deficit hyperactivity disorder (ADHD).

Dr. Hall Brown holds a Bachelor's degree from Duke University, a Master's degree in Clinical Psychology from University of Maryland, College Park, a Master's degree in Clinical Investigation from Johns Hopkins Bloomberg School of Public Health, and a doctorate in Clinical Psychology from the University of Maryland, College Park.

www.ingramcontent.com/pod-product-compliance
Lightning Source LLC
Chambersburg PA
CBHW060135100426
42744CB00007B/789